THE AMAZING ODYSSEY

How to unleash the best version of yourself

The Amazing Odyssey

Copyright © 2018 Jeff Dimagmaliw

ISBN 978-0-578-40509-4 (Hardcover)
ISBN 978-0-578-41374-7 (eBook)

First Edition

Published through IngramSpark

Ingram Content Group, LLC, 1 Ingram Blvd., La Vergne, TN 37086, USA * Ingram Publisher Services & Lightning Source, 52-54 St. John St., Clerkenwell, London EC1M 4HF, UK * NBN Int'l | Ingram Publisher Services, 10 Thornbury Rd., Plymouth PL6 7PP, UK * Lightning Source France, 1 Avenue Johannes Gutenberg, 78310 Maurepas, France * Lightning Source (UK) Ltd., Chapter House, Pitfield, Kiln Farm, Milton Keynes MK11 3LW, UK * Lightning Source Australia PTY Ltd., 1246 Heil Quaker Blvd, Unit A1/A3 7 Janine Street VIC 3179, Australia

1-855-997-7275 (US and Canada)
+44 (0) 808 1648277 (International and UK)
+61 3 9765 4800 (International AU)
www.ingramspark.com

Feather illustrations by Jun Dimagmaliw

Wing illustration by Sketchepedia/Freepik

Cover design by DS-j 2018

Table of Contents

Preface

If you discovered or inherited an uncanny ability—something so incredible that it could change your life by taking you to incredible places, achieve great wealth, attain endless happiness, and affect others around you—would you take it? What would you do with it? Would you use it to ensure your future success? Would you use it to help those you love and care for? Or would you teach those who oppressed you a lesson they'll never forget?

The Amazing Odyssey attempts to answer these and more. It will guide you through a journey of the amazing discovery of unlocking a power within you that you never thought existed or was even possible. It may sound strange and unimaginable at first, but it has been proven time and time again throughout human history and buried beneath layers upon layers of secrets. The path to it is to change your perspective and redefine what you thought was a limited way of thinking.

I was just the average person—working class, had a dream just like anyone else but didn't really make it my mission in life and just wanted to get by, pay my bills, take a vacation every now and then, although I could never explain why I always had an itch to know if there was more than *just this*. How I got started with this unusual quest almost felt like "it just came to me," not in a midnight dream nor in the musings from meditation or heavy religious influence. It made itself manifest in my thoughts, in my actions, and finally through the words in this book. There was always this part of me that questioned, "What purpose do I have? What purpose does everyone I come across in life have? Are we merely like ants in a colony or is there really something bigger we never fully acknowledged?" The answer came to me, little by little. It presented all these magnificent perspectives and experiences and all I had to do to keep the process going was to *surrender* myself to it, to allow them to just happen and for once in my life, stop doubting.

Everyone is born a genius at something when they realize they are. Everyone has the capacity and ability to become insurmountable, if we can only get past the illusion that we are only born average and unquestionably limited.

I took all the outdated rules in my life and set them aside. Things such as, "Don't speak unless you are spoken to. Keep your head down and just keep going by. Don't over-interpret something. Everything that has a scientific explanation is the only basis of logic." Amazingly, things just started to happen. To this day, I experience one amazing thing after another, I find myself looking at ideas from different angles and seeing perspectives the average person wouldn't normally see, and I find generous amounts of wisdom poured into my daily life—and I want all of these for you as well. This, I finally realized, is part of my purpose and my service to you and the future.

This guide was designed and written from the teamwork of both conscious and subconscious thinking. Roughly 90% of your mind that governs the decisions and functions you make on a day-to-day basis is from your subconscious. It is the conscious 10% of the mind that we exercise full control over everything else. As you read the chapters ahead, you will not only be able to discern which of the two is speaking to you, but it will awaken, if not compel you, to open your mind's eye to new perspectives that can positively influence your future's success, perhaps even help drive the next generation towards betterment. You will not only stand-out from the *crowd*, but from your former self, and you will literally feel your knowledge and wisdom grow exponentially.

I wrote the next chapters in full honesty and in believing that you will greatly benefit from their guidance and examples. This book has been written with no intent in misleading your beliefs nor to charm you with empty rhetoric. Everything came from the heart and from the mindfulness of someone who is free from ill will. You are the proper beneficiary of all the knowledge contained in this book and the rightful administrator of whatever you learn from it.

Our ancestors, who in various cultures we honor and respect, have a well-preserved way of teaching us ways how to cope with the difficulties of life and achieve success. They, however, never had the chance to enjoy the technological advancements we use today and the social interaction we are familiar with: the internet, social media, fast-paced business, followers and subscribers, innovation, cryptocurrency, online dating, and so on. There is no way they could've expected these and incorporate all their legacy knowledge to accommodate our present. Though one thing is common from their generation, to ours, and beyond—the inspiration to become successful and the ability to attain your goals in life. *This* is your chance to improve upon that and the guide to making it happen.

Prepare yourself for an amazing journey that will take you to places as close as in the incredibly complex multiverse inside your mind to as far as the endless wisdom the universe can offer. All within an *easy-to-understand* approach and guidance that will never push you to discomfort and leave you hanging there. As capable and amazing you are today, I guarantee you will be the far better person by the time you have gone through the journey. It is a trip I am excited for you! We'll start easy, and then we'll climb higher and higher until you begin to realize that you can go further without my help. Until you are ready for that level beyond, you will always find my conscious and subconscious here to help raise you every step of the way.

Thus, with full confidence, I say to you, "I know you can!"

CHAPTER ONE

ACCEPTANCE OF TERMS

"A thousand-mile journey begins with a single step" (ancient Chinese proverb).

Listen and believe.

What I am about to tell you may change not only the world you live in, but the world as it is experienced for others around you. It sounds profound, doesn't it? Maybe even incredible?

It could be because you currently perceive that your abilities and the senses that support them have practical limits. After all, isn't gravity what draws every object with weight towards the center of the Earth? Isn't the air that we breathe invisible to the human eye? Isn't the passing of time spent in seconds, minutes, hours, days, and so on? You know, however, that by reading this book, you don't consider yourself the average person. You're not willing to accept that you are a limited being and that you have profound abilities deep beneath the surface of what currently serves as the image you present to the world known as *you*. Indeed, you are smart, intelligent, and you are highly perceptive.

Let me ask though, "Where did you learn all that you know of the world? How did you come about accepting them?"

I do not challenge the fact that dropping a bowling ball on your feet would cause a significant amount of pain and damage, but I know you would not argue when I say that gravity is not the same on the ground as it is two hundred miles above the surface of the Earth. You wouldn't also challenge the fact that the same clear air we breathe is also capable of bending and changing light from great distances. Isn't it true?

Finally, you would not challenge that time is not just a measurement of the passing of a moment, but the journey towards a development. If you say that this is all about perspective, you are correct. If you say this is all about hypothetical ideas, you are also correct. If you say this is all about alternate realities, you are still correct. Then how come all these principles—perspective, hypothesis, and alternative realities—co-exist all in the same situations I mentioned?

The answer is, "It is possible because we have simply come to accept them as they are taught to us that way." It is not incorrect, these are indeed facts, but the fact is also that there are far more elements in this world than what we can ever define. The rabbit hole is deeper than we previously thought. Unfathomably deeper.

Let me be clear and honest: I do *not* intend to misguide your interpretation, that is simply not my goal here. My goal is to help you understand beyond what you know and perceive beyond what you visualize in your magnificent head so that you can unleash the power within you to be the best version of yourself and fulfil the best possible role you have for this lifetime. We are not just the ones to fill the top of the food chain pyramid. We are designed to explore the depths and heights of our abilities far beyond what we think we are limited to. Yes, there are rules, and if you really must, stick to the rules you know. If you want to discover what is beyond the individual that is you, then keep an open mind as you continue to read. You will never be faulted for your current beliefs on the practical rules in this world for they are what keep you in check, but it would be such a shame to simply limit yourself for what you were originally designed for. Fear not though, we can play by both rules.

Let's first establish common ground, some *pre-flight checks* before we go take-off on this *magical mystery tour*. Answer some questions for me:

Where are you right now and what are your surroundings like?

What do you do other than work and does it feel fulfilling?

How would you rate your quality of living and the individuals who contribute to it?

Do you feel at times that there *has to be* more than just the mundane *rat race* life you are currently going through?

Do you ever look up at the stars at night or stare at the ceiling and ask yourself, "What will become of me?" "Is better possible?"

The best journeys start where you look back where you came from and understand your point of origin as well as know which direction to start the trek. Give yourself time to pack-up for this amazing trip. Take your time, and take only the essentials, but be mindful that what you may bring with you may or may not be something you will need. It's possible you will bring something important only to toss it away in the middle of the journey or pick-up something along the way that you never thought you would pick up and miles into the journey, it starts to become an extraordinary thing. There are so many ways this can go, and that's alright because we're all different people. We have different paths and different experiences. We have these varying origins and varying goals to where we want to be or a mix of different definitions of who we want to become. We're each entitled to our own individual journey map completely customized for each person. Sometimes, our paths may cross. Sometimes, the paths become parallel with another person's life. Sometimes, we're forced to step back to step forward.

There are several amazing things you will eventually notice as you go through your evolution:

- You will have a guiding voice in this journey and it will sound exactly like how you expect it to sound. That voice will transform over time.
- Your perception on many things will attempt to redefine itself and it may be either challenging to comprehend at times or eye-opening and bordering between miraculous and ridiculous, but it is necessary, and you will prevail as long as you never give up
- Situations around you will start to change for the better and in accordance to how you perceive them, and you will find yourself eventually working

alongside these situations whether they are favorable or otherwise

- You will take cues from sources where you never thought was feasible
- You will grasp ideas that reshape the way you comprehend
- You will learn the art of letting go and whatever you let go will not haunt you or make you miss it, and it may in fact make you feel ten times better
- The development process will seem exponential for some, and *unfathomable* and *incredible* to others, but you will always know how to ground yourself and pause the cycle. In other words, "You're always in control."
- You will be able to look at yourself in the mirror and with good honest conviction say back, "I am you, but the better one"
- The old life you knew will appear dull and lifeless in comparison to what you are about to learn
- It gets easier and easier as you go along and practice

The biggest preparation for what you will need for this journey is important, and that is *acceptance*. Acceptance is knowing that you have a very steep mountain to climb and not everyone would be willing enough to climb it. It is the acknowledgement that you have limitations and rules, but you agree that you have to restructure them to make this journey possible. Acceptance is understanding yourself and the state where you start may not be perfect the way you wanted it to be, but you are willing enough to make that first step. You know something's wrong or you know something is amiss. Hence, you're reading this book and you want to go beyond your limits, beyond your current abilities.

But you are fearless enough to do it, aren't you? In fact, you owe it to yourself that you can evolve to a far greater individual capable of contributing the most amazing innovations and being able to become utterly amazing in everything that you do. Within each of us is a being that holds the keys to unlocking our own full potential. We also owe it to ourselves to acknowledge that it is alright to expand and improve and put those keys to good use. As I have said before, each and every one of us is designed for a purpose far more significant than we can comprehend. As simple as it may sound, a small spark is enough to get this radical transformation going. It'll make more and more sense as we go along, don't worry. I guarantee you'll be amazed at the results in the end.

Let's first accept that we're starting at *ground zero* here. This is our starting point, right now in *this* very moment. If you're truly honest about yourself, you'll realize that not every part of you is as ideal as you'd like them to be. But these parts still serve a purpose to us. They're part of us therefore they're important. But you know deep down that a lot of things about you could be made far better such as your whole outlook in life, your stability, confidence perhaps, your goals so far away from your grasp, and so on, are something you need to learn to face.

You deserve to be better and you deserve all these great things in life! Sometimes, what you may perceive as imperfect can be, in fact, something just *perfect* for your positive change. You cannot appreciate the stillness of the ocean until you have seen how chaotic it can get in foul weather, nor can you appreciate the warmth of the sun without feeling the sharp bite of a cold wind. They are all necessary just as contrast is necessary in a photograph. Technically speaking, shadows and highlights are as vital as shape and tint is to make what could qualify as a picture. In a slightly different perspective, a black and white painting can be as interpretive as the slight difference in tones in a clear blue sky. Imperfections vary in how vulnerable they make us, in how we perceive them, and how they serve each one of us. Therefore, you cannot compare your imperfections to another person because they simply cannot relate to it and it's pointless.

Do this instead: Instead of stating you have imperfections, look at yourself as the collective genius of ingredients that can create the recipe for making a bespoke ultimate version of you that you will ever become. Regardless of your perception, you are perfect the way *you* are made, perceived limitations and all. You are given the path that is never straight not so that you are put in front of discouraging challenge, but so that you may learn to use it to your advantage and see that it is a path and not a hindrance.

You have a limitless soul. You are the embodiment of evolutionary perfection craftily morphed and molded into the being of a unique role which is who you are today. You are a magnificent creation of infinite possibilities and capabilities and you are more than able and deserving of achieving greatness.

Exactly why you are here in this journey, right?

I joke about a person taking a Ferrari to the grocery store down a block to get a quart of milk. It's possible but not practical, though it's eerily akin to what I'm trying to say on how we have so much potential and we can do so much more but we may be underestimating the extent of our abilities. This is you, you are an incredible machine and though you are in no fault for wanting to put on a very expensive suit just to retrieve the junk mail from your mailbox, you are equally as entitled and capable of wearing pajamas to her Royal Highness' annual PJ Party.

There are so many ways you can slice and dice this, but the bottom line is that you are never bound by anything other than the rules you impose on yourself and the rules from other sources that you accept. Despite these rules, we are also given the freedom to choose, to create, to like or dislike, to have preferences. Ultimately, we allow the things we allow to come through the door whether it is by limitation or by choice. You are a person born with the freedom to react as you so deem fit.

Since Day One, you have always been free to make a choice within the limits of your environment. Regardless of whether you were born in a rich or poor upbringing, you've always had control over your own actions and decisions based on the reaction you got from something. For example, I'm sure you had challenging times in your life when you were growing-up such as trying to be self-confident after being ridiculed or judged. How did you react to that? Did you become angry or did you fold? You might've gone through the pain of a break-up. How did you react after that? Some may brush it off easily. Others take a very long time to heal.

Still, there is a choice that you can make from the most sensible and least compromising to the most radical and extreme. You could've either cared less about the people who ridiculed you or you could've made some damaging retaliations. You could've given yourself the time to heal from the break-up or you could've embraced anger instead.

The point is, you always—*ALWAYS*—have a choice no matter what happens to you. You are entitled to take a direction, or a response to a hurtful or painful event, and you can use it as the starting point where you decide to take a different route in life.

Everything has an origin; a starting point, whether it is measured by distance, time, or capacity. It is not common to find people ashamed of where they come from or how they started on a journey. Growth, after all, is a development with a series of decisions being made along the way that teaches us the preferences of what we like and what we don't like. Starting points also give us the choice of direction or where to go from there. When you draw a line, you know where it points due to an origin and the same goes for when you make a transformation in your life. If you are someone who dislikes your past or the background of where you came from, you can decide to move away from it or keep circling around it.

Sometimes, people get stuck in the origin and never escape the *orbit*; they can never muster the ability to make a decision. When they have something traumatic happen in their life, the pull of that trauma is so strong because they do not easily see a way out of it. Their perspective keeps circling back to that moment and they never move on.

Sometimes, it takes several cycles of "here we go again" before a person can realize that there needs to be a route out of that loop.

You may have heard before of the quote, "History repeats itself." It sure does. History repeats itself because its intention is for us to learn how to make things right or better, to break the cycle and starting a new course out of the old one. It repeats itself so that we can make a process better, to be wiser, be better decision makers. Until we can find a way to break a repeating occurrence, the occurrence including how we deal with it will always keep coming back to us.

How did you get to start reading this book? What prompted you? Reflect on these things as they're important in the journey because this is where you make a mark on where you started. If you have realized that your starting point was far before in the past, take a moment to reflect on that journey you've already travelled prior to getting to this point. For some, the past journey feels like an eternity, and for some, they barely remember the details.

Whatever whirlwind of a path that got you here, the important part is that you are here with me and contemplating the possibilities in your head of where this could possibly take you. Don't be afraid to look up and wonder. Set your eyes on the highest point that you can imagine who you could be after you're done with this book. Keep that gaze steady and you will not only visualize how far the road we have to travel together, but the amount of changes and fine-tuning we will have to make. Where it will take you is an amazing place and an amazing state of being. You will be completely different and far better than the person you are today, and the version of you after you're done will go beyond the limits of your imagination. You will be *awe-struck*. Consider this your pre-flight planning stage then. For now, just imagine the possibilities.

Seriously, take time, put this book down and just think for a while. Take all the time you need—minutes, hours. Whatever it takes, just as long as you do it.

"So, what is it like," you may ask. What is it like to become the person you strive for—the ultimate *superhero* version of yourself after mastering everything in this book and the specialized lessons crafted for you that you will discover for yourself? What is the end like?

Though it is hard to describe exactly who you will be, and I will no doubt generalize it for the sake of the audience in this book, I will tell you from my perspective that the version of you in the future is invincible from many things. You are invincible to the poking and prodding of the world, the people that instigate your emotions will have no power over you.

You will see a different perspective every day from the most grandeur of visions to the magnified details you have never seen before. You will be able to see for miles and miles and it will keep on going. Your confidence will *soar,* and that confidence will be noticed by those around you.

Situations will be kind to you instead of dropping problems on your lap. Life will unfold in many ways and it will happen right before your very eyes in which you will not only witness, but partake in.

You will become the master of your domain, your skills, your capabilities extended beyond the farthest reaches of your imagination. The ultimate version of yourself standing in front of the world unafraid, unshaken by anything that comes your way, able to create, improve, innovate, lead, and so many more positive traits unlike you've never seen or felt before.

Your perception of time and circumstance will expand. You will no longer be reactive but proactive when you engage in daily decision-making. Your emotions completely in control and unshakeable regardless of how difficult it gets. The definition of your character, habits, and preferences rebuilt to a far better standard and reconstructed in a way that improves your intellectual capacity to think and reason. You will feel like your memories and your future are working in tandem to solve any problem as efficiently and as straightforward as you can.

I know many of these things seem so incredulous and inconceivable, but that is *exactly* why many give-up so easily at this stage. They've chosen to live within the viewpoint and limitations from experiences and rules governing them. Where the line is drawn between the person who you are right now and the person who you could become is the belief that there is more to who you are and what you can do. That is the first step—to believe.

Believe in yourself, believe in the possibilities, and believe that there is a higher power watching over you and wanting you to succeed. Whether that power you define is God, the Universe, the source of all creation, it is all one and it manifests itself in so many ways that can be understood and viewed from countless perspectives. When another person declares that their perspective is the correct one and undermines another person's beliefs, that is where conflict begins. In common situations, the beliefs are actually the same though seen from two different perspectives. We will talk about belief in a later chapter. For now, let's focus on the more pervasive things happening around us.

Another difficult thing that affects us in today's modern society is that of many distractions. We are on social media far more than we should. It doesn't take much convincing to see that while you are waiting at a crosswalk with others, how many are hunched-over their phones looking at the virtual world that swaddles their egos and their self-perception.

Test this out, look around you when you are with the masses of people. How many are confined within their own tiny handheld world? Our thoughts are not built to be confined to something so narrow and something so useless in the long run; our thoughts and minds are created to go far beyond what self-image and *third-party approval* can provide for us. Promoting one's self-image just for approval can be petty. It is the kind of candy you toss in your mouth when you are hungry and the affirmation that never holds value over time. It tethers you to believe you are a person who is not important enough to become the incredible person you can be. Self-image doesn't rule you and you should never bow down to its fruitless promises of success and satisfaction. It is not the path you take to show what you can achieve for it does not take you far enough what you even begin to deserve to be.

You are more than just a person who *Instagram's* their food pics. More than just a person who likes to shake their fists on a public issue that has no bearing to their goals. The sad part is that so many people fall into this false sense of achievement today. Some may say it's just a fad of the times, but honestly, I don't see it ever going away. It will only change from one form of reckless needing to stand-out and get noticed to another form and it will only get worse.

Self-image is not the enemy here though, and in fact, it is rather important in this journey. It is only when it is used incorrectly and for the wrong results that it becomes a depreciating factor. If it's done to incite jealousy rather than inspire other people to become like you or better than you, then it is wrong. If it is used to repeatedly bash another person's view of themselves, that's obviously wrong too. If you use it in a manner to mislead someone who admires you by promoting someone else's ideal other than your own, then you become a sell-out instead of a role model. People of today may be smart enough to detect the subtle differences between what's real and what's fake when a person states their interests, but they can still fall into the same false propaganda. We can do much better than this and we are much better than this.

If you turn the channel on the latest news, there's plenty of attention-grabbing emotion behind the headlines. The way news is cast feels like less of a report and more of a show. Don't you notice that? It's there to incite and win your attention. When they switch to commercials, there's less information and more emotional stimulus. It's an old trick to grabbing your interest and one that's been used again and again. Lots and lots of glitz to skew our perception of something.

This is not what our perception is designed for, this is being tricked into accepting that our views are based on another person's instead of seeing it as an opinion of what is possible or allowable for us. We've been trained so much to behave this way to the point where if it was not presented this way, it would have no value. It's like drinking energy drinks for a few days and then suddenly replacing it with water. We get addicted to the level of excitement it gives us and expect it. When it is not there, we look for it. It's a great example of falling for the art of distraction and if not taken seriously, we could be numb, and it would be very difficult to know who we are anymore as individuals because we would all fall into the same trap.

In future chapters, we will revisit the power of calming the mind, being able to make peace with stillness and using it to tune-out the *unwanted frequencies* that try to get in our heads. Meditation is the new gym of the modern times. Sadly, the mind has been left behind with all the regimens we see daily and all the glamorous benefits of physical improvement: diets, six-pack abs, products that promise a higher chance of being noticed by someone you fancy, wrinkle-free skin, etc. The unwanted frequencies can be in the form of distractions that could make it difficult, if not prevent us, from being the very best version of ourselves in this lifetime. Calming the mind involves the ability to remove unwanted noise and unwanted stimulant or distractions so that we can focus on the path where we need to be. To calm it is to remove that curtain of uncertainty and replace it with common sense, uncompromising knowledge, and recover our connection to the power within us that gives us the means to be resilient and wise.

Here's another bad element of humanity these days— *Pride*. Today, we share the term for parades and marches we see on television, but the pride I refer to is the onset of self-righteousness that we brandish with themes such as, "We are better than you," or "Don't mess with us because we've been here longer," or in the lack of sportsmanship as, "Your team always sucks." We misinterpret pride as the over-appreciation we have for ourselves and the circles we belong in by making those principles rise higher in rank by putting opponents in a lower category. When we do that, it does not change the quality of the opposition, nor does it instill in their minds that we are indeed better than them. All we've done is rhetoric. In jest, this is acceptable, provided we know that at the end of the day, we are all equal in capability.

All of us are all born equally provisioned with the ability to choose and allow regardless of what corner of the world we start from. If you've lived or are living in a country of poverty, it's too easy to see that there are obvious limits everywhere such as the lack of food or comfort, but these are limits of the environment around you, not limits you impose on yourself. If a foreigner was to tell you that your life is worse than them, they would be ignorant; they cannot make a comparison simply because they have not walked in your shoes. Or sandals, depending on what part of the world you come from.

Some of the happiest people I've known do not need all the luxury we take for granted daily to keep them happy. Yet if these things are taken away from us—fast food, cellphones, the internet, shoes, a refrigerator, most of us would easily feel miserable. In this lifetime, you will realize that in some aspect of your character, there will always be someone better and somebody worse than you. *Always*. And at the end of this journey, you will have no need for pride for it will have little use. You will have nothing to prove to anyone of your accomplishments or abilities other than towards yourself and you will know deeply that you are comfortable with that because you will learn new things about you that naturally steer you away from petty attitude.

Speaking of parades, anyone who has the need to parade their qualities is insecure about something. Take bullies, for example. Bullies tend to need to be on top of the fear chain because it is where no one can see the flaws they're hiding or they're not confident enough to trust that other people won't undermine them. Any confident person who has nothing to worry about hiding anything does not need to exert any power over another person. Bullying is not a sign of strength, and neither are we to prove we are strong. We already are, we can all make a difference, and we can stand-up to anyone. Often, we just don't know it yet.

We already know that we are strong enough to be able to take care of ourselves and even others when it comes down to it. We can reason with our emotions to a certain degree and we are able to provide solace for our friends who had gone through a difficult time. Each one of us exerts strength in our own ways and we can become a great example of it to inspire others, to teach them, and to live harmoniously without the need to intimidate. This is what you will become. You will become a catalyst for your own strength and be able to draw strength from those around you and within you without assertion.

The next question you may ask is, "How long does it take? How long does it take to transform or to see results or to get to the mindset that we need to be to accomplish anything we could possibly want?"

This is a dangerous question because it poses the requirement of time to gauge the success. Much like distractions, we can easily fall prey into the all-too-common impatience. When we do not see results derived from an expectation, several things can happen. We can seek retaliation in some manner, to provide a justification as a means of compensation for the loss of our expectations. Retaliation can come in the form of employing unbridled emotions that may feel good at first but will grow into something that will introduce damage to us and our way of thinking. We may become discouraged into thinking if this is the right path or if we are still on the right course. The feeling of being lost in the process, any process, can give a sense of loss of control. For many, the loss of control on a situation or on a plan can become irreparable and require immediate soothing. Often, the soothing does not come from a clear state of mind and therefore distraction is employed to compensate. The worst response we can do to being impatient is to turn against our own selves.

"Why did I get myself suckered into this?"

"What the heck was I thinking? I was a fool; this is going nowhere!"

"This is nonsense, this is not right for me and I wasted my efforts."

It is all *too easy* to quit and to bail when things get rocky or there is no visible mark we can grab on to as the next objective. It is so common for many people to employ countermeasures when the discomfort of waiting sets in.

People in this age have become more and more impatient on results—we want things faster, we want things now, we want things delivered in a manner befitting our expectations, we expect this and that, we set the level of service that we feel is rightfully ours to take, we are afraid of waiting for anything longer than necessary for our oh-so-important agenda. This is not the way the world should work. This is not the way the world was made, and this is certainly not the way how we develop. How much of a quality do you expect to get when the effort put in to making something is hurried?

This is what I mean by the concept of time being skewed. We use it as a means to measure everything. To *God*, or to the *Universe*, or to *Life*, the concept of time is irrelevant if at least very different from how we use it. What matters most in this journey is *you*, not whatever time has passed. Time is the byproduct of a process and is also the unit of measurement people use when they cannot grasp the development of an idea.

There will be so much of this "time" spent as you go through this journey. Rome wasn't built in a day and thank goodness for that. Otherwise, Rome would not be the Rome we know now. It would've probably crumbled a long time ago from everything being half-baked. Time would've torn everything down or forgotten about Rome by now. Anything built in a hurry, whether it is an idea, a culture, or even a cake cannot be built quicker than it requires lest we expect a lesser quality version of it. Face it, process takes time, evolution takes time, and perfection requires your steadfastness over a period of growth. I know you can do this, and I know you can set the concept of time aside and think beyond the typical definition of time because you are beyond typical. In fact, you are supernatural, and although our minds will never fully grasp every concept of every aspect of us becoming supernatural, we can certainly get a taste of it and we can develop the mindset that fosters this way of thinking.

It is all too easy for us to be discouraged especially that our society is now familiar with the repercussions of everything. Not everything, however, meets the same repercussive response. In fact, most are overkill. For instance, not being popular leads to tendencies of being behind in the social ladder. Not being productive gets us behind an agenda that we've built. Not being strikingly different from the next person could put us into the category of ordinary and thus prevent us from being noticed. There are layers upon layers of this that can get rooted deep in the human psyche. It's all too easy to feel that we are worthless and that our frame of being is so fragile that it requires a lot of maintenance.

We are *better* than this, better than to succumb to the musings of discouragement. We are better than being roused to think that we are lesser in value. It is upsetting to know that a being of perfection and potential such as yourself can be subjected to this kind of trickery. The entire evolutionary sequence created from the most complex of orchestrations with the ingredients of the universe crammed into a single being, coerced by the idea that he or she will never be good enough for anything.

The stupidest idea anyone's ever created is one where it belittles the capacity of humanity to achieve better than they are able. Have you noticed that the wisest of our scholars have never said anything that makes us seem so small? All of these *quotes of wisdom* you see flying around in social media vouching for you and subliminally attempting to get you to kick the bad habits of thinking and being (ironically on an addictive social media platform).

Discouragement can lead to so many undesirable results and can be the big elephant that squeezes you out of the elevator going up. Like a cancer that branches-out into different parts of your life unbeknownst to you and by the time you realize it, it's spread into every part of what you do. Everything we do is in a huge part done by subconscious thinking and decision making such as going through the motions of doing laundry while talking to someone over the phone, or the faint soundtrack that accompanies us when we read, or that built-in editor that arranges the words in our head milliseconds before we are about to speak. If we have trained our subconscious that we are not worth the effort or that something is too hard for us or that something cannot be achieved without all the sufferings and failures, then we have been fooled and have taught ourselves to fail. The actions and responses of one—if you are still wise enough to notice—will be of one who always finds a struggle with everything that comes his or her way.

Discouragement is the devil's henchman who tells us that we are not worthy of success and that we are best doing far less of what we were designed to do. Discouragement tells us to put this book down and stop. Discouragement whispers in our ear to tell us that we are not *the brave generation*, that we are not strong, that we are no better than a simple chemical reaction. It clings on to the best parts of us hoping to run us down and strives to keep it that way. So be brave and face the challenges.

Be strong! For deep down, you are so capable of becoming something great. You *always* have been and *always* will be.

Just like there is much discouragement everywhere, there are many forgotten sources of inspiration and means to rally the mind and body. The first thing to shake the bad things off is say, "So what?"

Dust-off that reset button, which, by the way, you have unlimited resets in this lifetime and you can keep hitting that button for as many times as you wish. If you're stubborn, that reset button gets rusty and gets difficult to press. A person with the agenda to fail has thrown away their button. Gone. Out the window. They don't need it. They believe that life is a game where the amount of retries is equivalent to the amount of lives they have— *One*.

Failure is obviously not an intention but facing it allows us to develop strategies that would otherwise remain part of our solution portfolio. Failure allows us to correct the course dial and re-train our coping mechanisms and reinforce our keel so that when we encounter the same situation, we can do better. As I said before, "History repeats itself so that we are given the opportunity to make it better." So, press that reset button and then find the responses of encouragement around you. Don't wallow in the results of a failure. Think of it as an avenue on a map that you now know leads to a place away from the goal you are trying to get to.

I came upon a tree one day in late winter. Its leaves stripped away, looking like it had been sleeping and looking lifeless in comparison to the same version of itself during the summer. Despite the cold weather, it still stood there, arms stretched out in wait for warmer temperatures. As the seasons started to change, the tree started to sprout tiny leaves and flowers. All the while, bees and other flying insects were orbiting the tree as if encouraging it to grow and busy pollinating it. Birds were picking-off smaller insects off the tree, with each flutter purposeful in some way that made the tree shake its branches. The sun comes, gives it warmth and energy, and starts the next chemical reaction of life. Yet the tree has no knowledge of the birds, the bees, the sun, or the mechanism behind them, only that it is an undefinable part of its cycle. Eventually, the tree matures, its leaves thicken, and it starts to bear fruit. The fruit eventually fall on the ground and provide for other creatures that dwell underneath it.

Just like the tree, there is encouragement all around us we may not be aware of that sustains and promotes our growth, and in general, this is how the universe works. It comes in many forms and delivered in many ways that can be unique and bespoke to each one of us. Each one crafted specifically for our growth and betterment regardless of whether we see them or not. Our own interpretation of them becomes the language they use to communicate to us. When was the last time you felt the warmth of a hug? Do you still remember the positive reverberations when someone last gave you an encouraging pat on the back? Have you come across a bakery that drew you in because of how good it smelled from the doorway? These are little things, little hints and such. Yet they can be profound when it is you that gives them the meaning.

The universe will provide for you. God will provide for you. *Everything* in between you and heaven will provide for *you* in this journey. Your job is to *trust*, to *understand* that, and to *accept* the terms that you are in absolute charge of becoming the utmost person you could ever be, and that life will always find a way for you for as long as you do not lose hope and especially the faith in yourself. For losing faith in yourself is losing everything that stands between your current state and greatest version of you.

Take some time to reflect on this chapter. It's a lot to take in and your mind could be swirling from either the possibilities if you're feeling optimistic or doubt if otherwise. I highly suggest taking some quiet time on how this chapter applies to you. Think about it but please, don't be discouraged. It gets more complex as we go along but things will unfold and make sense. You will never be alone in this journey be it from my guidance or the path that led you here, and you will not be lost in your development for you have this guide as your map.

CHAPTER TWO

PATIENCE

Everything in nature has a cycle of transformation, we know this very well. We can regard life and death a cycle as evident as the tides or the exchange between day and night or even far away when our planet rotates around the sun. Sometimes, the transformation has a repetitive cycle—things repeating *over and over again* such as water evaporating and coming back as rain.

Sometimes, the change is linear but parallel, meaning the transformation commonly happens to many things but does not repeat. Occurrences such as the transformation from young to old, from a journey's beginning to a journey's end, the life stages of a butterfly. Whatever the pattern, they all require the development from one phase to another and it takes time. Unfortunately, time is something that many people misunderstand.

In the previous chapter, we talked about how time is irrelevant to the universe; to God. One cannot comprehend the development of the Earth to the now living organisms on it including you and me by the mere counting of time as much as one cannot comprehend the time it takes for a life to take hold for someone. Time, though a unit of measurement towards an amount of development can also be misinterpreted as "waiting for a result."

This *waiting* is where the disconnect is. Waiting for many people requires the mundane checking and re-checking of a status to see if there is movement or change. If used to measure ourselves, we can be subject to some harsh judgement. I am not downplaying time itself. We need time as much as we need room to grow, but we do not use time as an expectation. The destination of a journey should be the expectation. The change that happens should be the expectation. Not the time itself that accompanies it. "But it's hard *not* to count when one is waiting," you may say.

Of course. We are all trained to count, and we are all trained to wait. How else would we have learned patience? But patience is not the waiting game that many commonly define. Patience is much more than the holding back of an action until a desired situation has occurred. Patience is more than controlling one's emotion when something doesn't happen their way. When it is said that patience is a virtue, it means that patience is a quality of high moral standard. It is an action of nobility and maturity to react in such a way where an expected behavior is looked upon by understanding and high intelligence. When someone is trying to learn how to ride a bike, does the instructor measure the success based on how long the person has ridden the bike? Or does the instructor measure the success based on how effective the person is using the vehicle?

Don't be fooled when someone says, "You have to be patient," as a way for them telling you to stop bringing up how long it's been taking or stop asking how many more miles before you get somewhere. Exercising patience is *not* the suppression of time. It is the self-encouragement of one's involvement towards a transformation. To exercise patience requires one to be able to handle mistakes not as punishments but as learning tools. It requires one to be aware of the contrast of how something has started and taking that into account the underlying process and challenges that come. It is the dismissal of the idea that we are not fit to improve in this life-changing journey. Patience is not being hard on yourself no matter what happens.

It is very important to *never* be hard on one's self. You can certainly push yourself to your limits to hone a skill or get to the next level of success, but this does not require beating one's chest to crack the proverbial whip from within or even going to extremes to destroy a part of our selves. We are masters of our bodies and decisions, yes, but we are good masters. We are not ones to drive ourselves to the ground so that we may rise. We do not grind ourselves down to a pulp just to rebuild a better version. We should be our best friends in this journey and in this life. When we fall, we have to allow it and face the pain that comes after. However, it is wrong to punish ourselves with negative feedback or constantly berate ourselves with negative reminders to never fail again. We will only grow up *hating* the person we see in the mirror and that will cause us to get stuck in an endless loop as well as extend the same treatment to others.

No one has ever benefitted from another person who pushed us to the limit using down-facing unwarranted negativity as an answer to failure. If we have ever succeeded from it, it may be because we've known that love is stronger than hate even if the only people who love us the most is the person staring back at us in our own reflection. I have no doubts that we will stumble and trip during the next chapters. But we need them, we need those lessons. We need the perspective and contrast to know something we like that works for us and something we don't like that pulls us back from progress. It will always be a difficult lesson to learn from indeed, but its saving quality is because it is not easy to forget. So be prepared; get those *spiritual Band-Aids* ready. You're *gonna* need them!

Breaking old habits is not about literally destroying a part of ourselves unless we can see that those unhealthy habits will inevitably lead us to our demise. We have to be wise and attentive to what we feel. Our feelings give us direction jut as our gut instincts tells us whether to do something or avoid it. Feelings are among the most powerful inspirators to our growth, but it can easily be distracted, coerced, bent, and deceived. If a feeling of absolute positivity graces us, it is not easy to deny it by design. It makes us feel good, it surges endorphins, and it creates good memories. In these same positive feelings, there is insurmountable amounts of momentum that allow us to achieve what we desire. This is why having a clear conscience coupled with a powerful compelling feeling and confidence in one's self is a superior catalyst to becoming successful.

Along with the journey to the successful you, I will be helping you eliminate as much negativity in your mindset as possible by teaching you ways on how to banish them for good. There are other factors that can pull us back in this trek such as: the lack of forgiveness, despair and hopelessness, anxiety and fear, pride, pressure, anger, hate, and indifference. Notice these are all qualities that mainly affect the spiritual side of us and not physical?

The physical body will *always* follow your mindset. If you are happy, the pain becomes tolerable and you become set in a state of calmness that contributes to healing if you are injured. It's been proven scientifically that a person who has a positive mindset heals faster and endures stress and that a pessimist is plagued with issues. Even the way we treat animals, it's the same way. And if you've heard of the Japanese researcher, *Masaru Emoto*, and his findings on how negativity and positivity affect the molecular structure of water, you'd immediately understand what I am talking about. He made an experiment where a glass of water was subjected to positive verbal feedback and another with negative and found out that the positive water had a uniform structure under the microscope whereas the one subjected to negative words was all out of alignment.

This is even true with an experience I personally have from a small laurel twig. For months, I had such a small twig sitting in a tiny jar containing no more than an ounce of tap water. It would stay by my bathroom sink unexposed to any kind of sunlight or fresh air. Every now and then, I would add more water from the tap when the level would go down. About once a day, I would whisper a mix of positive encouragement to it.

I would say, "You're doing great! We're going to be just fine! You are special. Believe in yourself."

This went on for several months receiving nothing but positive words coming out from my mouth once a day while it sat in the dark for 95% of its severed existence. It was still green, the leaves pliable and healthy, the stem as fresh as the day I found it, and the water even without changing it for weeks never smelled foul nor did it discolor. I was already convinced at the second month of doing this, but I just kept it going. To this moment, I continue to give it kudos. It not only taught me that there was sense and proof in *Emoto-san's* experiment, but that here it is right in front of me telling me that it's not just the water that positivity can affect. If we can influence elements by our intent and provided feedback, imagine what we can do to ourselves at a much larger scale if we give ourselves the same encouragement! It's endless energy and we are the conduits.

> *"Not only are we in the universe, the universe is in us. I don't know of any deeper spiritual feeling than what that brings upon me"* (Neil deGrasse Tyson).

We all came from the same energy that created the world and every day we receive that same energy in many forms be it physical, spiritual, or mental. The conduit of endless streams of energy in this unfathomable and bountiful universe—that is who you and I are.

Let's take a moment to reel ourselves back in; catch our breath. We are taking about patience after all. Patience is also about practicing holding back and not be in such a hurry to get things going. Please do not mistake it for *procrastinating*, that is different. Procrastinating is the lack of focus on a desired outcome and using time as a vehicle for a distracting excuse. When we procrastinate, we ultimately delay the inevitable or allow parts of our plan or the entire initiative to fail. It pushes our momentum to the side and we end up doing more work trying to get the ball rolling again.

Pausing to reflect is a pit stop, a checkpoint. There is no rule as to how long one needs to pause to gather focus, reflect, and re-adjust the aim, but you must be able to keep the momentum going during the wait. If you set it aside to let it become stale, you will lose interest and may eventually toss the whole idea down the garbage. This is not what we want to do. Practice catching your breath to revitalize your senses and to give yourself the chance to see things from a different angle when you are trying to grasp a concept.

As I go through my year, I often reflect on checkpoints— events within the year that break the monotony—such as weddings to attend, a vacation that I've been saving-up for, upcoming movies to watch in the theaters, even places to eat after a long busy weekend. It's a brief hiatus that refreshes the mind. Opening the windows after the air has been stale in a room is a great analogy.

What are things you like to do to take a breather? Whatever they are, use them not to escape the process, but to reset the stress level that may accumulate from it. In today's busy times, we forget to pause and get our bearings; we often charge forward with lighting speed, sometimes even on the reckless side. I see it all the time. Take traffic when going home from work as an example. It's so easy to get caught in the hubbub that the impatience turns into other things such as frustration (*#&@$%!),

anger towards other motorists ("Come on! Pedal to the right!"), and hopelessness ("This traffic will never get better, and here I am still needing to get groceries.") and the sad thing here really isn't the reaction because it's only natural that when we are in an uncomfortable situation, we want to release the pressure somehow.

The sad thing here is that as we go through this state of being, it becomes engrained in us subconsciously. The ways we cope with difficulty become a *natural* part of our behavior and it makes us difficult to reason with. Over time, it stems into other traits and next thing we know, we get to a breaking point somewhere down in our lives.

Here's another example: working in a job you've been doing for so long. Have you been waiting for that promotion? Have you been working your butt off that you're so frustrated with your co-workers who aren't picking up their own weight? Not making an impact or climbing up the ladder yet it's only been a couple of months? We've become so focused on attaining overnight success and instant gratification that we fail to realize that the faster we go, the easier it is to stumble and bruise our egos.

Are the breaks you take considered productive or are they considered distracting? Think about this for a moment because there's a very thin line between a productive pause and a distracting deviation. Both are necessary in the process.

A productive break is one where you keep the momentum going even though you've put it on hold, like keeping the engine running as you step outside the vehicle to take a photo of the scenery. The idea of the process is there sitting in the back seat of your priorities as you use the time to let things sink in or the time to find a different angle prior to re-entering the process when you're ready. It's a "happy pause" where it's as comfortable to stop as it is to continue.

A distraction is slightly different. It snaps you out of the process and you can even put the process on full stop. A distraction is used when you are uncomfortable in the process and need to relieve the pressure badly. However, it becomes a fork in the road that will always ask when attempting to get back on the saddle, "Do you want to continue?"

Some are healthy habits, others are just time-killing mechanisms. I find that walking is a great method of pausing, especially if done by myself. I get to listen to my own feedback echoing in my head and I get to have full control over what I want to use as a topic during the break. Plus, walking or just even going outdoors when the weather is nice is inarguably a great contributor to your physical condition. If I want to distract myself, I will do something that will take my mind off the subject completely such as going on social media, watching some TV, or playing a game. When I'm done though, I find myself stopping before the doorway of the process and try to lure myself back in.

Be mindful of these *pauses*. They are necessary but if you find yourself pausing excessively, something in the process probably isn't sitting well with you. Try to identify what they are by having a conversation with yourself—an honest, no-holds-barred, I know your deepest darkest secrets, so you don't have to B.S. me kind of conversation. We'll be having more of these through the journey so get used to being honest. We'll also be going through how to get the best out of these conversations. Long ago, when we saw someone talking to themselves, people thought the person had a loose screw. Nowadays, when we see people talking by themselves, we assume they're on *Bluetooth*.

Kidding aside, this process will no doubt take a significant amount of time in your life. I don't necessarily mean it will take years but that it will be a part of your life that you will no doubt remember. The universe was not built in years but countless eons, yet its product—*you*—were built so quick in comparison.

Does the universe care how long it took? No. Its definition of time is beyond how we comprehend time. You are the process, the nerve ending, of this amazing evolution. If you are so eager to find out how long it will take, then *by all means*, skip to the end of this book (or *any* book for that matter). It will make little to no sense when you get there. It's not about how quick you can turn your life around for the better. It's about how successful you are in making that change.

Just as the universe continuously unfolds, so will you. You and your mind will never rest, that's just a fact and it's not a bad one at that. Not until you've had your last breath will you finally "rest in peace" as the saying goes. From now until then, we will create, we will improve, and we will try to unleash the best version of yourself living beyond your imagination!

Go ahead and take a break. Put this book down and let this chapter sink-in. We will continue whenever you are ready.

CHAPTER THREE

LETTING GO

"The illiterate of the 21st century will not be those who cannot read and write, but those who cannot learn, unlearn, and relearn" (Alvin Toffler).

We are creatures of reaction. We react to all sorts of stimulation whether it is a product of provocation or one of inspiration. When we see clothing that we like displayed on a store window, we light-up, we are attracted to it like moths on a flame. We are like greyhounds on a race track when the bell rings to announce that school is over. We salivate when we get a whiff of our favorite dessert. As we were kids, when the ice cream truck was close by, you knew it made your heart palpitate in excitement. Wait... It still does? That's alright, I'm not judging.

As we grow, we encounter more stimulation, more reaction, and we store all of these in our subconsciousness. Here's a test: Think of an evening when you're sneaking into the kitchen late at night. Amid the darkness, you grab hold of the refrigerator door and pull it open, hoping nobody hears you. The refrigerator light slowly pours out of the door and spreads to illuminate the kitchen. "There it is!" You reach out for the glass jar of marinated wet pickles and begin to open that jar slowly. You hear the *"thwop"* of the lid as it slightly depressurizes, and you pause ever-so-slightly to make sure no one heard you. No one did? Good. The smell of sweet brine oozes out and you fumble one pickle out of the jar. You get ready as you sink your teeth into that sweet juicy pickle.

Is your mouth watering by now? Exactly what I mean.

It's a reaction driven by the subconscious to a stimulant that presents itself by... Wait, what?

You want to get a pickle?

Seriously, you want to get a pickle?

Now?

Fine, go get a pickle and come back. Make sure your hands are clean.

As I was saying, we're easily driven by stimulation. The problem is it's everywhere nowadays, even in places where it shouldn't be. It seems that everything is practically screaming for our attention: The food we eat has a lot more sugar content now than it did before. The insurmountable number of ads that we see on shows and they battle for your attention in hopes you don't turn the volume down or press the Skip button. The news we read is full of fear-inducing and comment-provoking traps. It feels good to troll in the internet for some. Video game controllers have more buttons today than a telephone, and games have gotten so complex that their objective is to completely immerse the player until their bladder can no longer hold more urine.

This isn't all that reprograms our subconscious. When we grow-up, we are taught about the basic life-surviving skills and we learn from the toughest lessons because they are new to us. Most parents want to see us succeed in life and sometimes, they dump buckets of anger and frustration that each time we get doused, we redefine ways of coping with it. In extreme cases, we get punished with levels of unnecessary pain heavier than what can be considered a justified repercussion. We get our hearts broken more than we hoped it wouldn't. We become embarrassed when we are ridiculed or when we become the laughing stock of what could've been otherwise an uneventful scene. And the lessons we get from all of this, layers upon layers upon layers that build-up over time, is what we use to protect ourselves from being put in a similar unfavorable situation again. The most vulnerable side of us locked away and defenses up, often so thick that very few to none of our closest friends or family are allowed in. It becomes a security blanket or a shield to protect us from the tiniest pebbles that bounce off to the large boulders that try to get it to massively crack.

We live in a society where we are so well-guarded that we have assumed that just about everything we are exposed to, whether it is people or scenarios, wants a piece of us somehow. It's borderline paranoia in a pandemic scale, and yet it's the new *norm*. It's the acceptable character that walks among us in society and the irony of it is, we want to make things better.

But how can we make things better if we continuously live so guarded? So seemingly invincible?

It's simple:

1. We consciously observe the reaction we have from the lessons we've learned in our lifetime, one by one as we encounter them.
2. After we have reacted, we recall the reaction and scrutinize them to determine if they were justifiable or if there could be a more efficient approach to dealing with it.
3. We rewrite and learn the new improved lesson and exercise it in every opportunity.

Aren't we *still* the masters of all our decisions from the grand to the miniscule? So why then would we not be able to take those same decisions apart and upgrade them if we see a chance to improve? This journey is all about improving level after level. If we cannot give ourselves the honor of accepting a reconstructed update to some old habits, then we will be on the same loop of being the same version as we were.

Whenever we react to something, there is an associated history behind that specific behavior. We learned it from early on, even the basic components of the reaction may be based on a collective of other lessons learned in the past. That's how we adapt, we take *Lesson A*, combine it with *Lesson B*, and we get *Lesson C* as a new formula. Generally, when we learn something early in our lives, it becomes the blueprint of how we define our character. When we grow-up, we retain those lessons, and we remember them. We base new lessons from old ones and the evolution takes place. Dogs are far easier to train when they are puppies. Children's minds are like sponges. Much of our early beginnings are designed to catalog our definitions and mechanics. We immediately learn what we like and what we don't like and then formulate a path around them. The map of our subconsciousness, being drawn and detailed in every step of the way.

If we are fit to be the wise people we are, we will realize that there is an eraser at the other end of that pencil. Whatever we write, we choose to make indelible, but that doesn't mean it is there for good and we cannot erase it. As long as we are aware that lessons can be unlearned and made better, there will always be a chance to improve. This goes on for not just matters of the subconscious sense but also of the physical. What do you think was going on in the head of the person who discovered that depression was not a spiritual disease but a chemical imbalance? Imagine the treatments for it before versus the treatments we have for it today. At the time of this writing, there are numerous discoveries about treatment plans, drugs aimed to eliminate the symptoms and experimental ones to target the source, and more support groups and research teams around the illness.

It is possible to improve a system and people who have an open mindset are the ones who often find the ways. If we are not able to let go of past theories, there is no room to develop new ideas. If we cannot be willing to unlearn some of the lessons in our life, we cannot find room to evolve. Prior to contrary belief, we are not stuck with the cards we are dealt with and there is always an opportunity.

Opportunity is the best gift life can give.
Take it or leave it, the choice is always
yours.

The hardest part is learning to let go of past lessons and have the wisdom to rewrite them if need be. You may say that these lessons helped you through life, through the most difficult of times even. But I am not asking you to reconstruct every single lesson that you've learned. I'm asking you to be observant of your lessons and change the ones that have not been so effective for you or the ones that you know deep inside they could be better. Sometimes, you have to change them and sometimes, you have to let them go.

Speaking of letting go, we will learn how to get better at that technique, lighten the load, and replace old habits and knowledge with better components and smarter systems. It'll be just like overhauling and it's another difficult thing to learn just like patience. But we're not done yet. This is just the beginning. Fear not, you're doing just great. Keep it steady, pace yourself for you are the master of your own schedule and take breaks to let things sink in.

CHAPTER FOUR

LOWER YOUR SWORD AND SURRENDER

Because we've learned so many habits and lessons that have been carved sometimes deeply into our minds, letting go can be difficult to many. But when you start to get a hint that things could be better and that you could be exponentially greater than the super calculating human you are, you'll see that there is a benefit. Letting go is not about giving-up habits and *giving-up* is too jarring of a word. Letting go is more about being able to disengage and separate the conscious into two or more perspectives in order to get a clearer understanding of how the entire mechanism works.

If you can let go of a heated argument between you and another person, for example, you will be able to see the issue from a different angle and re-formulate a better strategy. It may allow you to see how ridiculous and determine if you may be over-reacting to the situation or just fueling the fire even more. You may even be able to take control of the argument by diffusing the tension or apply a technique where you shift the attention of the subject as an attempt to mitigate it or lead the conversation exactly where you want it to be. If you have suffered a heartache, letting go can be a very useful tool to preserve what is left of your loving self and move forward and cope.

When we *disengage*, we obtain the ability to tug on our own leash and provide self-control. We are able to correct our course and steady the boat when the waters get rough. Because we are surrounded with so many things we can react to it can be refreshing to know that if we are able to stop the slide down into a reaction, the tables turn, and we start to take control. Every argument I've seen escalates because one person is feeding the other person's emotional reaction to the unpleasant yelling and arguing. The argument becomes a competition of who's louder or who's got better come-backs as opposed to working on a solution.

This is immaturity at its finest that we can be drawn into a low-level pissing match. In another situation, operators in suicide hotlines are trained not to escalate and be able to diffuse a heated talk between them and the people who call. By taking control of the emotional temperature, they are able to draw-in the caller to come to their level and have a higher chance of being able to get the caller to see things from their perspective. That's how we win. We do not allow ourselves to easily give-in to any emotional poke and prod and therefore we do not easily get fooled nor do we get drawn down a path that could be to our disadvantage.

Remind yourself every now and then to observe all the stimulus around you. There's plenty in newsfeeds, in advertisements, in sales pitches, even in the subtle ambient noises you hear around you. Sometimes, the stimulus is not intentional, but you can draw your own decision on how you want to feel when exposed to them. You'll feel this when you walk by the beach during early morning. The gentle ambient light as the sun just begins its way upward and the waves that caress the sand you walk on. It puts you into a state of calmness and relaxation, doesn't it?

Sometimes, the universe talks to us this way especially in nature. Nature is the language of the universe for it is directly associated with anything that is not synthetic. When you are in a crowded place such as an outdoor market—all the yelling and the crying of children who don't want to be there and the constant bumping. It makes you react differently. When you read something funny after visiting your favorite social media outlet, you get drawn into wanting to see more because of the endorphins that contribute to that emotional state. In short, it's everywhere, but that's okay. It is what it is and the only thing we can do about it is exercise awareness so that we can try to control and be conscious of how we react to them.

You may say that it is easier said than done. And if you do, then you may have inevitably set the first limit upon yourself to which you have to overcome. I like the word "surrendering" as applied to this chapter, as in *surrendering* to a higher power or a bigger cause or simply allowing things to happen but being able to filter them as they come. By surrendering, you are allowing the healing process to occur and that is what eventually leads to rebuilding, and reinforcing, and better response. You are also showing yourself and others that you appear wiser and very stable-minded. And remember, there is a difference between *surrendering* and *giving-up*. I don't ever want to see you give-up.

You may have heard of the phrase, "The Art of Allowing." It is a method to which you allow all situations to happen especially if you have no control over them. The first thing you must realize is that everything that happens around you leads towards your betterment. It all points back to you. Even a tragic loss is something that you can learn from and teaches you how to reinforce your coping and response mechanisms. Trying to take control of something inevitable is a total waste of energy. Your energy is better spent on planning what should happen beyond the inevitable occurrence. If we are smart enough to realize that there is more to an event just than when it happens, we can see beyond what the typical person sees, and we can make the appropriate adjustments to our behavior and in properly dispatching the damage control department. That's the point, right there, and most of what this book really is about—to be able to see beyond what you see and be able to act upon the numerous situations that arrive at your doorstep so that you can gravitate and produce the best outcome from that opportunity.

The best decisions you can make are those that are not heavily influenced by a negative emotional state. If you make a decision while you are angry or sad, you are likely not thinking straight because most of the effort in planning the next actions become biased towards removing the emotion and not the problem. Why do we sometimes make rush decisions? Why do we sometimes feel like we want to punch anything we can put our fist through when we are angry?

Our reaction to tending to the emotional wound is profound and if not properly administered can become the goal of the issue. There are people who become trapped in that state, sometimes for the rest of their lives unless something earthshaking happens again and they find themselves nursing yet another emotion that takes them even further away from the original problem. It can go the other direction as well. Being overly joyous and *drunk from laughter* can mask something unforeseen. I don't advise you to use a completely null sentiment when planning for that would not give you a sense of satisfaction. I merely say, "Tone it down," and just make sure you have a hold on the reins when the horses get *wild*.

One very important note: When your emotions become too overwhelming or you find yourself extremely difficult to control them or they affect you so much, seek professional help. There are trained people familiar with your emotional imbalance and are educated to formulate a plan to help stabilize it so that you can have better control of yourself. Seeking help from these professionals is *not* a weakness in any way nor should it be associated with your pride. You have to accept that something is wrong, and you can be in a far better state than you are.

In one fateful time in my life, my cousin, who had been with me in many adventures in the past, finally set a date in December when he was to get married. The wedding was in the island of Maui in Hawaii. What a perfect setting, I thought, everything that I loved about nature packed in a long-awaited weekend. The wedding day itself turned amazing not only because of the quaint location of the chapel where it was held nor the following happy reception nor the comfortable weather, but just finally seeing my brother-at-arms tie the knot and solidify his own adventure with the woman he loves. Though the wedding only lasted for one day, my family and I spent the rest of the other days going around the island, visiting beach after beach, killing nothing but time in the most relaxing ways we could find.

One late afternoon at one of these locations, I found myself lying down enjoying the warmth of the sand while I watched my two nieces frolic by the shore with my sister. To my right were my mom and dad sitting by each other just talking away about all sorts of miscellaneous things, my brother-in-law out in the water. It was such as beautiful and peaceful scene, almost dream-like in a way. The kind that made me sit up straight and get a grasp on how everything was just right and well-presented by the world before me. The sun was slowly starting to descend, and I felt it was time to take one more dip in the water before getting ready to head back to the hotel. I got up, walked to the water, and paddled my way to my brother-in-law, bouncing in the shallows as the gentle sway of the waters helped me be light and buoyant. A few yards out, I caught-up to him with the water already up to my chest. He was just staring into the distance to where the island of Lanai was.

Without losing his fixation at the horizon, he said, "Isn't it just beautiful?"

My brother-in-law was born in *the Big Island*, but it was evident he never got tired of seeing it again and again. I understood immediately how everything was completely in accord with each other—the sky in hues of orange and yellow, the large island of Lanai floating in the distance, the nudge of the water as it embraced me, and the gentle breeze that repeatedly *kissed* my forehead. It was captivating and awe-inspiring, and it was inevitable to think how fortunate I was to receive such a spectacular front-row view of the ethereal present.

I responded back, "Yeah, we're definitely lucky to be here."

After a minute or so of gazing, he said he was going to leave and head back to shore to dry-up and pack. "Alright then," I said. "I'll be there in a moment," and he proceeded to swim back to shore.

I stayed in awe absorbing the perfectness of this slice of time where I found myself part of the immense world and the world being part of me. The newfound perspective was colorful and hypnotizing. All I could think of during that time was how I got there not in the physical sense but in the events that led me to the state I was in, namely the emotional state of gratitude.

Whenever it is quiet, the mind is compelled to speak with such volume that it elevates your senses and attempts to open your wisdom on every known aspect. All my successes in life were there, as were all my failures, my career choices and co-workers who shaped my knowledge in the industry, all the people I missed so dearly who have left for the next life, and the ones still here who have abandoned my heart. I had never felt so alone yet so connected at the same time yet the absolute intersection where they met was exactly where I needed to be. I looked-up to the heaven so wide and unsealed that it filled my peripheral vision as vividly as it did in front of me.

"I am listening," I said gently like a little child looking up to his grandparent.

What was remaining from the doubts in my head started to make their final plea: "What am I doing?" I thought. "This is ridiculous, I am talking to no one! What's the point? Am I just having one of those over-emotional moments again?"

This was different, however. The synchronicity was so perfect I felt that I was under God's spotlight, and I don't believe that anything happens by coincidence. There is always a purpose to everything and everyone.

Without a single word uttered from the vocabulary, I quickly understood what it was trying to tell me clearly and the reason why I was summoned: "Everything will be *fine*. I've got you. Trust me and let go. Just let go!"

I felt my hand open and my arms slowly raise, first a little to the side, then they lifted a bit more, and more, the higher up they went, the farther away doubt became. Up and up until they surfaced from the water.

Finally feeling the most vulnerable side of me exposed with nothing to hide, my outstretched arms showing the world every part of my being, I uttered in an unsteady but sure tone what I should've said many years ago:

"I surrender!"

I never realized how much weight from all the heartache, all the missed opportunities I beat myself for, all the anger from people who mistreated me, the rage, and the sadness had been hiding all this time. For the first time, I felt a release from a grip that held me for a very long time and the bridge between me and the universe connect and come to an agreement.

To say the least, it was perhaps one of the most profound times of my life, those simple few minutes in the water that lasted what seemed like an eternity. Finally, I began to heal.

What *exactly* happened here? You've most likely had a similar experience where you were compelled to respond to something you can't explain. It varies from one person to another in terms of *intensity,* but the overall lesson is that in several points of our life, we will experience a moment where we question ourselves, "What am I doing," and it is up to us whether to respond to it or brush it off as just another occurrence. But to those who fear being laughed at or ridiculed at the idea of responding to such a beckoning, I say to you, "Don't give-in to what you think others may think of you. Don't *especially* think that by responding to such a call, you will start to doubt your own sanity. Your own sanity is a reflection of what you choose to accept."

If you truly desire to become the *best* version of yourself, you will dismiss any notion that you are only limited to certain avenues that are rational and acceptable to the general masses. Remember that we have learned as a collective the ideas and rules that give a generalized sense of what is acceptable and non-offending to as many people as possible. Our goal is not to offend, of course. These days, anyone naive enough to think their values are better than those from other individuals with different experiences and different upbringings will be easily offended. To be offended about something is to limit one's self of the ability to adapt and be resilient. We cannot entertain the idea of what could potentially be better, or even the best solution we may come across if we are not willing to be open to other views and other perspectives. If you chose to live your life afraid of the consequences of being judged as someone who employs methods that are not practically acceptable to the masses, then perhaps it is they who are missing out on the opportunity.

You can always reject ideas just as much as the next person, we are given the free will, and nothing should ever be forced down the proverbial throat of your mindset. You are always in control of what you chose to allow in, block, or banish. Do you think that by learning ways to improve, you will rid yourself of your old values and you will feel involuntary to whatever replaces them? Of course, not. As I have said, *you* are always in control and you can take it or leave it. What I offer is a view in the mindset of your future potential as someone who can bring change to yourself and maybe even the world. We are not zombies; we are very much alive and aware with the same opportunities and unlimited number of blank canvasses we choose to paint on as the next person.

It may come as a relief to you that at first, I was in denial about my change. Who wouldn't? When something completely different comes your way that takes you by the hand and says that you can become better and I will prove it to you, you will instinctively bombard it with doubt. Understandably, the doubt is there to protect us should we think it's a scam or it's a trick of some sort. Doubt was taught to us the first time we were fooled as kids. We no longer want to be naive or easily laughed at. Though if you are old enough to read this book and visualize the concepts, you are also mature enough to know that parts of this make sense and that there really is something that can be done to get away from the rat race and be the advanced culture we were meant to be instead of struggle frequently to achieve success and attain the respect, recognition, and reward we always look for. New ideas are always not easy to accept, but they are not impossible.

Let go of your doubts and your defensive habits and give a new perspective a chance. Give it the chance it deserves to show you the better life and the better you. A culture that has no need to be afraid of what happens or invoke superiority if they are in the same room with one from a different culture is one that is highly advanced.

If doubt is a defense, then ignorance is its people. To act superior against your fellow man or woman is to doubt the solidarity of your own moral character. The only person acceptable of receiving your show of superiority is your former self; never others. When you show others that you are better than them, you lose respect and credibility. A person of power does not need to show it to gain respect and leadership qualities, but to help others realize they can also attain power. And should they eventually attain it, there is no reason to fear feeling less superior for each of us will always be different in how we define superiority or inadequacy.

By now, you can see that the objective of this chapter is so that you can be mindful of your beliefs that hold you back. Whether they are based on fear, doubt, inferiority, or just being ignorant, they can represent themselves in so many different ways that can discourage you. Though it's not always about believing that self-betterment is the solution, there are other humanistic traits that also prevent us from being the best we can be. We may easily believe that we can be better, but we can also hold on to sometimes painful lessons in our past that can derail us just as easy.

Take for example, someone who has wronged you in the past. There are plenty, I'm sure, we all have them. Whether they be old classmates or a bully at school, a friend who misplaced his or her loyalty to you, a co-worker or boss who didn't think you were fit for a job, the love of your life leaving you for another, and so on. Some have been long forgotten and brushed-off, others may have been excused and an agreement has been made to go separate ways, others may still be here to this day visiting your thoughts. It's especially hard when we are taught how to recover from these wounds especially if the ones to give them to us are the ones we care about. This is perhaps one of the hardest lessons of all—*to forgive*.

CHAPTER FIVE

FORGIVE, BUT NOT FORGET

*Forgiveness is humanity's most difficult
feat.*

It is the lack of forgiveness why people first learn how to feel hatred against another and why wars spanning for decades, even centuries, continue to smolder. Depending on where we came from and our upbringing, forgiveness may not have been among our first lessons, because our survival depended mostly on being tough, stop crying, and never be oppressed. From the somewhat rough place I grew-up from, it wasn't something that was even considered other than during sermons from our local priest or Sunday school. It's unfortunate that the extent of forgiveness is sometimes even associated with weakness or submission towards an offender. But the truth is, forgiveness is the tool of the elite and when used properly, can heal both the trespasser and sufferer, and inspire witnesses.

It is all too easy not to forgive and that is what makes it even more difficult. Today's expected human reaction to a push or shove is to shove back (or even strike back). It takes *massive* mind control and wisdom to forgive. But let us not define forgiveness as a last resort or an optional course of action. It is in my opinion, a selective decision to the recovery process of an altercation. We can forgive but we must also be wise and not forget. Forgiving is not the same as forgetting and moving on as if nothing happened, for doing the latter would be both illogical and ignorant. We can move on and still get along and co-exist, yes, but we can also wise-up as to not fall into the same cause of the tiff to begin with. Pretending that it didn't happen would allow the possibility of history repeating itself and things could be worse the next time around.

With forgiveness, *time* is your friend. Time heals wounds, it allows the dust to settle, and it brings about much-needed time for perspective and planning. The benefit you get from learning to forgive is unfathomable because it branches-out to so many other avenues and teaches you so many more things that stem from its grace. It separates you from a person who simply reacts for the act of forgiving requires forethought as well as recollection, both needed towards the wisdom of weighing the consequences, duration of the misalignment, and the development of peace and order. If we forgave all, it means we also remember all but we do not use it for the sake of being superior. Again, the role of superiority as discussed in the previous chapter applies here. Every chapter in this book is connected.

Let's start with something relatively easy. Recall a childhood time in your life where you were somehow wronged by another person your age at the time. Was it something that happened during recess? Was it something that happened while parents or guardians weren't looking? Was it something that took away your dignity or embarrassed you? Whatever it was, you are far from that now. Very far. And as the grown-up individual you are now, you are much wiser in knowing that it will never happen again because you are not only obviously older but because you know how the situation would've panned-out had you applied your knowledge now to the person you were before. I want you in your head to think of that moment and recall as much as you can from it.

Where were you at the time?

Was there anyone else there with you the time that it happened?

Do you remember as much of the play-by-play sequence on how it happened?

If you were able to stand between your younger self and the other child, what would you have done to mediate it?

If you were the parent of the other child, how would you have corrected the action so as not to scar the child from the wrongdoing?

If you were to rewind the clock to that moment again, how would the young version of you have reacted to avoid or remediate the situation before it happened?

Now that you have as much of a vivid recollection of the incident as you can, tell your younger self to forgive the other child. Even if it just feels like pretending right now, do it.

...And now, how does it feel? Do you think that the act of forgiveness would've changed not just that moment but other similar moments following it in the future? Absolutely! Do you think it would've made the child that offended you think twice about what just happened? Of course, it was a rather "grown-up" thing to do what you just did, he might think, certainly thinking years ahead and appearing even unshaken after it was over. You would've contributed to a new approach to future problem solving as your younger self grew-up and so would the other person. Any witnesses to the event would've likely learned something, too, in some level. Perhaps even any grown-up who was there at the time would've learned something from you, too. As you can clearly see, the ability to forgive spans beyond just the incident and it has the means to reshape the future whilst freeing yourself from unnecessary pain and worry.

Yet that was just a simulation of one thing that could've happened when you were little! Imagine if you were to transpose this in octaves—older age, more complex problems, how you react and use wisdom even deeper than the previous, so does the effect of forgiving transpose. Forgiving is a living organism capable of multiplying, creating waves of influence, adapting to adjust to the situation, and one that spans time and distance. Isn't that better than pushing the other child down to the ground? An action like that too can spread. But it does so in the opposite direction and with negative exponential results.

When we forgive, we take upon the act of *freeing ourselves*. We decide that we shall no longer be influenced by the negativity that came from the other person. We empower ourselves by removing the behaviors and reactions that otherwise bind us and keep us from becoming invincible, calm, and all-knowing. We can stop a disease in the mind from perpetuating and creating new diseases and infecting the good areas. The part of our conscience and subconscious that once contained the inability to forgive can now be home to a better idea that displaces the old tenant. Forgiveness is difficult because of our inability to realize how immensely empowering it can be. It is difficult because we often go the easy route and just react *tooth for a tooth and an eye for an eye*. It is easier for us to level with the offender than to go perpendicular, away from the arena and into a different plane of thinking.

If you may notice based on our previous exercise, forgiveness is not two-sided. You can forgive someone now before they even know it or even if the person is no longer with you. Because their offenses can often stick long after the deed is done, that person who has offended you has made a seemingly indelible mark. You can forgive someone to release yourself and remove that mark now or erase as much of it as possible; you don't have to wait when you're in front of the other person.

Starting the forgiveness by yourself completes a significant amount of the goal and reduces a great stress that you may not know spreads to other parts of your subconscious. When you forgive, it frees you from a poison that taints your spirit. If you find it difficult to move on with life carrying a guilt or anger, imagine how much energy you spend dragging that weight around. You may not feel it in the physical sense, but when you are freed from a bond, you never notice the difference it does to you. You become so used to the weight that it becomes part of your normal life and that weight could be used instead as something that should otherwise lift you up.

Pride will try to get in the way of your attempt to forgive. During the first stages of the exercise, it tends to appear frequent. Your challenge is to learn how to identify it when the feeling of forgiveness becomes hard to swallow. The previous chapter talks about letting go and this is how it applies towards this chapter. As mentioned before, everything is connected to one another, but being that we are limited to learning in a linear fashion, we have to read a book from left to right instead of from simultaneous points. It would be easier the latter way, but we are just not designed for that kind of thinking. At least, not yet.

I cannot stress enough how important it is to allow yourself to see different perspectives of the same subject, and to visualize the numerous ways a situation could pan-out. This is different from plain over-thinking. To over-think an idea is to apply unnecessary effort towards the solution of a problem. If you over-visualize, you would tend to go beyond the intention of the visualization. Though if there ever was a time to over-think or over-visualize something, it would be towards the numerous ways that things could go wrong if you did not set aside your pride to forgive someone.

And where does pride come in to your benefit? Is it to prove to the other person(s) that your ideas are righteously correct, and *they* are wrong? Is it that by silencing the possibility of forgiving, you are somehow preserving the integrity of your values? Be very honest with yourself and ask if your pride is worth the price of being unforgiving and if your actions to refuse the healing will likely involve others and deepen the hole. Any arrogance or pride you hold will prevent you from giving true forgiveness, and it is exactly in ratio with the quality of freedom you wish to give yourself. What you give is exactly what you keep.

If anger loves a reaction, misery loves company. True nobility is to exclude yourself from what is negative so that others may not be affected by its channeling through you. If the world knew how to forgive and practiced it, we would be living in peace and harmony that would span for generations. Imagine a version of you that can easily let go and be able to use a mature reaction when someone crosses you. That version of you can see beyond emotions and remain completely stable and precise with your thought process. Imagine a community with that mentality. Imagine an entire nation. Imagine generations with an evolved way of thinking and superior decision-making capabilities. Letting-go, forgiving, it all starts there too.

Anything that you do, provided you do it repeatedly, will eventually feel natural. Anything, whether it's learning to ride a bicycle or learn a different language or practice forgiveness. If you practice the ability to let go and not give-in to emotions, it will feel natural. And if you continuously practice the mindset of one who is confident, determined, and trusting, it will feel as easy as breathing. First, we will learn how to let go and forgive on a larger scale. Once we master that, we have to seal it with practice and re-learn the mindset so that it will never fade. We will learn the latter part on the next chapter.

When in times where you are not distracted, set your emotions aside. Be indifferent not to the people who did you wrong in the past, but to the hurtful emotions those people caused you. Again, think of another person in your past you remember that gave you a difficult time. Be there in that moment and like before, try and mediate the situation with the better, wiser, emotionally-unshakeable version of you

Unlink yourself with the younger version who received the offense and say something to the lines of, "This is far more important than retaining this hurt. You no longer have influence over me because I have decided in full awareness and commitment to move-on and release not only the hurt that you have inflicted, but what I have inflicted upon myself and others from not being able to let it go and forgive. I forgive not only you, but I also forgive myself. I pray for you so that you can find peace and recover from whatever has stemmed from this instance. I forgive you and may you live the rest of your life in fullness wherever you may be right now. May you be happy and spread happiness and may you spread the blessings of this world everywhere you go."

This is what it means to pray for your enemies and to be wiser with your actions. To fully embrace the ability to see past the judgements caused by the response from the emotional distress. To pray for your enemies is to liberate yourself and any negativity associated with both parties. Again, find another person. Say your own prayer for them if you wish to use your own words—as long as the intent of the prayer does not contain anything conditional. Forgiving someone requires you to do so unconditionally, and in doing so, you will also give yourself unconditional freedom and love. You have every incentive to forgive as much as you would want to be forgiven for your trespasses on others. The release and peace of mind is incomparable to anything you will feel.

Before you embark on another trip down memory lane to find the next person that has wronged you in the past, make sure that you have made peace with the previous individual. You may need to say another prayer or with a calm sense of understanding attempt to mediate the situation again and allow yourself to see an even wider picture of the issue and how it could transform into other problems. If you are unable to provide the ability to fully forgive that person yet, then come back to it later and think of someone else for now. There is an unlimited number of attempts to forgive especially when the offender has caused some serious pain that isn't easy to just shake-off. When you have made absolute peace to the point where thinking of that individual no longer triggers any hint of bad memories, then you have healed that part of yourself and you will notice other parts of you change for the better. It is much like severing a diseased branch—all the other smaller branches that stem from it, leaves, and all— also die.

As you go about your cycle of recalling people who have wronged you and forgiving them, you will find it easier to breathe and think. You will experience a sense of maturity and freedom of mind that you've never had in a very long time. The liberation you empower yourself with will create space for good things in its place.

Continue this process until you can find it difficult to recall anyone you can forgive. Once you have, the next people in the future who attempt to wrong you will face a much different version of yourself. He or she will see that your character is not easily broken, that your reaction to their offense will not provoke you, but instead cause you to take better action and stop the negative from spreading. Remember, you become wiser with each forgiving, and in turn will become further and further separated from the emotions that contribute to the pain you carry and encounter. You will be able to let go of the pain, the debilitating sadness, put anger in its place (anger has an appropriate place and time), and move forward beyond just one step in healing.

I know this should go without saying—be mindful that the idea of forgiving is not only a unilateral view of the people who have wronged you, for we too have offended others, and we will likely do more in our lifetime. It's important to exercise humility because humility will give you a great perspective on how you present yourself. It is not about self-embarrassing or lowering your head to demote your status. You can be humble and still exude dignity, or you can be proud or overbearing whilst unprincipled. Humility is a grace bestowed upon us to keep ourselves in check and appreciative of what is around us. When we know and understand that we are also capable of being in the receiving end of forgiveness, it becomes second nature to avoid hurting others, and that it never happens again nor spreads. This is how we move towards a more perfect state; the wiser version of being human, one that acts closely in sync with the spirit that is within us and making the situation ultimately to everyone's betterment. We never do this with the primary objective of gaining the upper-hand against others, but we do so to take the advantage against a situation that can ultimately turn against us.

In general, it becomes easier and easier to forgive as you train yourself to let go. It goes from difficult, to tolerable, to acceptable, to normal, to expected. You will feel invincible from the petty jabs of others and resourceful with all your social and ethical judgements and reactions. There will be times you find that you get stuck in allowing yourself to forgive someone. There are offenses that others that have done to us that we may consider unforgivable.

I should caution that although you may have to face your choice that you cannot forgive one or a few extremely grave offenses by others, be mindful that you are locking yourself also in that deal. If you are unable to let go, you will be in the same philosophical room with them for as long as you are unable. It will live in your heart and in your mind and it will haunt you depending on how tight your grip is. I urge you to find a path, a compromise at the least so that it does not detract your forgiving to something that is conditional. For these very serious matters, seek the help of others who understand the situation but see it from a different perspective; one that is unbiased. We have many chances to make things right and most of them start within us.

> *"To err is human; to forgive, divine"*
> *(Alexander Pope, An Essay on*
> *Criticism).*

Although the humanistic side of you is what makes these actions happen, the divinity within you—the omnipresent God that lives inside every one of us as well as the qualities he exudes—is both your guide in this journey and the part that fortifies you as you forgive, let go, and move forward. Yes, you have a divine version of you living inside you. It is the same soul that departs your body after you expire that lives alongside you right at this very moment. The question you have to ask yourself sometimes is, "What would that spirit do in this situation? It needs no body to defend, it has no use of grudges, and it has no restrictions on what it wants to be or where. It is a free entity if it wants to be. What would it do?"

Sometimes, the issue of being able to quiet your mind so you can focus better, whether it is finding the means to recall these people or just to silence the soundtrack that keeps playing in your head as you find the proper mental alignment becomes a problem. If you find it difficult to "tune-out" of the distractions and "tune-in" to the peace within, we will cover that in the next chapter.

Put this book down after this chapter and let it really sink-in. Practice what you have just learned. Go easy on yourself. When you are ready, the next chapter will be here for you. Remember, forgive others as you would want to have them forgive you. The pardon you give is the pardon you get, and what pardon you detain is the pardon you also do not deserve.

In time, it gets easier and easier to forgive and let go because you gain the wisdom and the value of doing so. You will realize that if nothing negative sticks to you, you are able to heal very quick or won't sustain any damage at all. Your mind and body will become inhospitable to negativity and thus the common oppressive or offensive things you find will have minimal to no lasting impact to you. Negativity will have no reason to dwell within you and can no longer infect your abilities to make decisions or think.

As with all things, it takes practice and practice and practice. Aside from learning to forgive, get used to being resistant and not immediately knee-jerk reacting to any provocation that would otherwise lead you down the path of needing to forgive. Learn to say, "Whoa, hold on there now. Let's settle this like grown-ups." Be *infuriophobic*; the trait for arguments and irks to slide off your back with minimal to no effort much akin to a drop of water on a lotus leaf.

"Like an oily duck," as I used to say in my earlier years.

Once you let it slide-off, it becomes a lot easier to forgive.

CHAPTER SIX

MEDITATION

If we ever jumped into a time machine and meet someone from the early 1900's and said that what we ran as part of our exercise regimen, we'd probably get a laugh at the least or a "You 'future people' are crazy" brush-off. No one would think that it was an effective way of losing weight and keeping fit. But just like that era, we might get the same reaction now in this day and age if we said in response to "What do you do at the gym?"

"I meditate," you would say.

If you think of how many types of physical exercises we go through; just about every inch of your body is affected by many routines, there isn't much for the mind other than meditating. Meditating obviously does not produce results that show in physical proof, but you will notice that your behavior, demeanor, and reactions do change. The more you meditate, the more these results become evident. It's true though. Meditation is an art that at present now gets excluded in the list of physical activities for a number of ridiculous excuses and myths:

- The world is full of distractions, finding a *meditation zone* isn't practical these days
- We believe the "no pain, no gain" mantra
- Meditation is only for monks and hippies, maybe hipsters, and possibly anyone with a long white beard
- It takes too much time to meditate
- It's more for the slow and elderly and not for the young and fast
- You need some thick religious background to pull it off
- It doesn't do anything; it's a waste of time and effort
- It's so easy, just close your eyes and say, "*Ommmmmm…*"
- It would make me look weird and socially unacceptable if my friends and family knew
- *Blah, blah, blah,* quartz crystals, *blah, blah, blah,* gluten-free vegan tofu, *blah, blah, blah,* Jedi Kung-Fu circus training…

It doesn't matter. People will find excuses and that's fine because ignorance is bliss and we're here to differentiate ourselves from the ignoramus.

We all have a spirit within us and that spirit lives as part of the experience we go through called life. If we do not give it the proper environment (including our body and mind) to thrive like a plant, it will wither, and it will break. Its metaphysical weight and mass are so dense that it can affect us and everything around us like a gravitational pull. To find the perfect setting of focus, we first have to start looking within us.

Peace is something we can spark from within, and the psychological mechanics of our species is designed to cultivate and perpetuate it. If we are imbalanced and conflicted with our thoughts, there is no focus and therefore no progress. If we can be exposed to environments where it is loud and chaotic, we have control of how we react to it, therefore limiting or allowing the growth of serenity inside. What we experience day to day is an interpretation. What we see, what we hear, smell, taste, touch, everything is translated, and we react to it. If it's a beautiful sky or a warm bath, there is a reaction to it that ultimately affects the way we choose to be calm. If it's toe-tapping beat or a thrilling ride in a convertible, it also gets translated and gives us a sense of satisfaction we can only explain as "fun." These are reactions to a stimulus.

What about stormy weather? Like I said, it's a matter of interpretation. Some people like the stormy weather because from their perspective, it's a great time to bundle-up indoors and read books. Some think that stormy weather is scary because of thunder and lightning. Again, it's an interpretation, it's a way of allowing the reaction to occur and choosing which reaction in our catalog to employ. So, to find the perfect place of relaxation really varies from person to person. Quiet places are generalized as good places to attract calm in the mind because majority of us would react the same generalized way. While others may find it unsettling due to the lack of noise, it is designed to see exactly how noisy it is already in our heads even before we get exposed to the lack of noise.

Always remember that anything you place in a supportive environment will have encouragement to prosper—think of how that fact applies to you.

Peace is a state of positive being. In a calm environment, meditation lets us tap into our inner selves. If you find it uncomfortable to be in a quiet environment, try turning off one distraction at a time. Turn off your cellphone. Perform a temperature check—how do you feel? Get some perspective and think of whether it is necessary or not.

"Is not having my phone on going to derail my stability?"

If so, then do it gradually rather than abruptly. Put it on silent at first and try not glancing at it. If you've mastered that simple feat, try placing it far from you. Then eventually, to another room. Try mastering that again. Then turn it off when you can let go. If not, repeat the challenge. Do this for other distracting elements too, such as closing the windows, or thinking less of what chores there is to do, problems you had in school or work today, etc. Like a carnival shooting range, pick them off one at a time.

Make this gradual transition from having distracting elements to calm if you find it challenging to just jump into the low-energy state we're trying to get to. Again, practice makes perfect. Don't rush yourself to a pace faster than you can handle, but also don't be afraid to challenge yourself. Never be too hard on yourself on anything you have difficulty accomplishing because it will only add on to the frustration. Forgive yourself. Move a little bit more. Let go. Find the calm. Repeat with gradual effort until you get there. It's the general law of persistence that ultimately, you'll eventually get what you want for as long as you keep on doing it.

Find that quiet place. Perhaps in your room provided you've got no distractions or are in complete control of every element, perhaps somewhere remote outside where you cannot be interrupted. There are no firm rules, as long as you know how to compare a calm lake versus a raging sea. It is important to have this calm place so that we can have focus. We'll be doing things in this mode so that you can modify the way you feel. Sometimes, it will feel like you've time traveled or passed through solid walls. Sometimes, it will give you a warm fuzzy feeling inside, and sometimes you will feel the release of pain and shed a truthful tear. But don't be afraid, you will always be in control, I promise.

The benefit of this entire exercise of calming the mind and meditating is that it gives you focus and alignment. Focus thrives in the absence of uncertainty. Alignment occurs in the absence of conflict. When both are applied, it becomes the blueprint of unity between you and your subconscious. You want to be able to easily get messages back and forth across your subconscious because your subconscious sees far beyond your physical and practical limits. It is the gatekeeper of all the possibilities that you can manifest and the representative of the ultimate version of you. Therefore, it is your trusted friend in this journey. The conscious part of you is the executor of your actions as agreed upon between your conscious and subconscious, while the subconscious is the planner and visualizer. When there is an accord between both your conscious and subconscious, you find the direction you need to rendezvous with whatever it is that you are trying to achieve. The direction is what leads you to the overall location and state of the desired outcome. That, my dear friend, is why this is so important.

There's no question that your mind is an *extremely* powerful tool. The most complex supercomputer design in this universe right there sitting behind your eyeballs. And what do we do with it? Good heavens, what do we even expose it to! It's common knowledge that we are severely limiting its capacity to create, influence, and its abilities to change the future. We might as well use a chainsaw to slice room temperature butter. The key to solving world hunger is probably in there somewhere. The next Einstein or Beethoven could be buried deep between your brain's neurons. The culmination of the most successful versions of you in this life lodged somewhere in the recesses of your noggin waiting to be discovered. I am not saying that you will be all of these, but I am not saying you cannot be either. To get the best versions of you out, we need the elements of focus and alignment so that your subconscious can tell you—in its own way— how to get there.

There are many points of entry into the meditative state. This is why in the previous chapters, we've been busy *cleaning the attic* and getting rid of things that can pull us back or discourage us. We need a clean frequency, the cleanest possible to operate in, so that when we commune with the subconscious, the exchange of information is not muddy and is easily understood. When we enter the essence of calmness, we must be properly set-up to get as much effectiveness as we can out of the experience.

Granted that the idea of meditating is to clear the muddy waters, it becomes easier when you get as much of the muck out before easing yourself in.

Meditation has been incorporated in so many parts of history. The fact that it has survived the centuries is a testament to how useful it really is. The earliest recorded teachings of meditation came from Asia somewhere around 1500 B.C. though that is not to say that Asia had developed the only form of meditation through the centuries. Prayer itself is a form of meditation, which is an open channel of communication towards God and heavenly entities, and if done correctly can also provide a sense of peace. Even listening to the sounds of *Mother Nature* such as the ocean or rain or the forest can make the listener feel that he or she is part of a larger being. The core of meditation is to sync the mind into a higher plane of thought and a re-alignment of thought patterns. It organizes your way of thinking so that after you come out of the meditative state, you can introduce a new perspective towards your usual ways of thinking and reacting to a situation. The calmness is not just about removing unwanted noise or distractions, but it is also to get distance from the synthetic influences we experience daily. The advantage of this is that when you begin to think, it is much less chaotic and more focused. You don't easily get distracted and you can become so focused that you can write an entire book without making much effort. Things flow so easily in and out of your brain and it does so in a way where it does not confuse you. There is less conflict, less hesitation, more wisdom, more confidence. Imagine applying this way of thinking at work and how much more productive and efficient you can be. Stress has no hold on you and you are able to set it aside instead of carrying it around (which could also affect other non-work-related tasks).

If you have never meditated before, I will share my technique with you. I know that this is not the standard way of meditating, and sometimes it may not work for some. Others who may be familiar with meditation could take this as a guideline. I know that there are meditation centers and groups who go on the deep end when it comes to this exercise and they take it with religious reverence. But with this, we will focus on just ourselves. After all, we *are* our own retreat center. Plus, we're on a budget and this is as cost-effective as you can get. Take my example though as a reference point of where your own customized meditation can take you. You'll also see step-by-step on how I personally get into my meditative state.

So, back to that quiet room. It is preferable to have a comfortable seating position when meditating. Lying down may cause you to drift away and sleep; we obviously don't intend to do that. Find a good pillow to sit on. Sometimes, you can opt for a meditation pillow which you can straddle between your legs as it props you upright. If you prefer doing your meditation outdoors, just be aware of your surroundings. It's preferable to have privacy and minimal distractions coming from Mother Nature so be mindful of where you decide to be still for the duration of the meditation. One technique I would recommend is something called "Grounding" (sometimes also referred to as "Earthing"). Grounding requires you to be barefoot or in physical contact to the earth with your skin. Some people claim they become in-tune with the energy coming from the soil and feel a sense of *belonging* with a larger entity such as the world itself. Some claim it has healing abilities that are beyond scientific explanation. Personally, I find it liberating much like my feet in the sand when I'm on vacation. Perhaps that's why we get that unique relaxing feeling in a tropical getaway different from an oceanic cruise. Grounding to me is also an act of humility and a symbol of membership to something grand, accepting that we come from dust and to dust we shall return, hence the feeling of being at home and able to freely express myself. Once you feel safe, no one will bother you, your phone is on silent mode or turned off, and there are no heavy visual distractions that will try to catch your attention such as people outside the window or cars passing by, then you can start to focus on your breathing. Breathe slow and deep and in a comfortable pace. Keep your eyes open and just breathe. In and out, in and out, breathe. It's just you, no one else, just you and the steady tempo of inhaling and exhaling. Do this for a good minute or until your focus is no longer concentrated on your breathing and it blends into the background.

These next parts will be a bit tricky because it will involve you closing your eyes. If you can, remember the next steps. Alternatively, you can record yourself saying the next paragraph using a smartphone app and play it back. If you live in the dark ages, ask someone patient enough to be with you in the room and help you by reading the next paragraph slowly and pause after every sentence (they can exit the room quietly afterwards).

Slowly close your eyes.

Keep your breathing steady.

In and out, in and out. In. And Out. In. And. Out.

Get used to the lack of vision. Your other senses will most likely heighten such as your hearing and your sense of touch, and your mind will no doubt be looking for something to think of. For now, focus on my voice.

We will start to mute the other senses starting with your sense of touch. Place your hands on your lap and keep them open but relaxed. If you are outdoors and grounding, feel the earth, feel the temperature, the very subtle vibrations of the soil shifting underneath your bare feet. You are connected to the world like a plug on a wall socket and you are part of the grid as the rest of the world passes by unfazed.

Relax your shoulders. Relax your arms, your hands, your fingers. Notice them loosening and being an extension of your calmness. Your appendages belong to you and they follow your order.

Let that relaxation sink-in. Each limb as if fading away into stillness.

Breathe in, breathe out.

With your eyes still closed, look up front. Steady your eyeballs. Do not let them move too much.

Visualize a point where you can fixate your eyes to. That is your rock; your steady grab in the void.

We will now focus on the noise. Let the miscellaneous noise that you hear, whatever ambient noise it is, let it all congeal. Let it all blend with each other so it is one noise. Everything you hear is one muted noise of nothing but ambience. That is life just passing by.

We will now get deeper. Keep yourself relaxed, keep your focus on that imaginary point in front of you.

Next, feel your presence amidst all this endless amount of ethereal and spiritual space. There is so much room to roam around you, so much volume you can fill. This is your space, the extent of the volume is you. It goes for as far as you can imagine. You belong to that space. You *are* that space.

In this space, you are in full control of yourself and all that embraces you. You are free to think, you can do no harm, you control the thermostat, and you own it.

At this point, you may find your mind trying to settle and feel aloft, but your conscious thoughts will fight it. It's okay; let it fight, let it try and take control, but the weight of your focus will be stronger. You will take the distracting thoughts and as they grow weary of fighting for your attention, you will pull them down, away from you.

You have a steady line of thought and you are connected to the stillness. You are one with it and you are in complete control of your new environment. No one will harm you here, in here you are safe.

Nothing else is welcome in your new realm other than goodness, and you are one with that goodness.

If your shoulders and arms start to feel some rigidity after getting some focus, relax them. Relax you face, your lips, your forehead.

Keep your breathing steady and calm. Feel the unity of your thoughts with the silence for there is peace in silence. Peace is with you.

Stay for as long as you want, for as much time as you need. You are free here. When you start to feel that everything has settled: your thought patterns, your tension, your worries, let them all melt away in the stillness.

…Relax.

When you feel this peace, when you feel this free-floating sensation, you now have focus and full control over your thinking. You have unity within yourself and you are holding the hand of your subconscious. Your frequency, the way you communicate to your subconscious, the universe, and God, is clean and clear.

There are two ways you can go now—One way is to use this time to detoxify and relieve the pressure caused by any stresses using this mode. You can use it to suppress any stresses or realize that in this space, they have no control over you; they will not succeed if they try. The second is to use this focus to now think of a singular problem you have affecting you in the present and use the calmness to find the solution. I cannot tell you what the solution is for it is rooted deep in your subconscious. This, however, is the point of the meditative journey where I cannot take the lead and you have to find it within yourself, in your own language, how to interpret what your subconscious is telling you. It is talking to you not in words necessarily, but it may even be through certain emotions. Words are beyond this meditative state. You communicate in this state through a language far beyond words can clearly articulate. When you introduce the said problem in this state, you remove all emotions as you present it. Think of the meditative state as a dimly-lit room where there is a spotlight on the issue, and you look at it from outside your own perspective, as if the issue is not yours but someone else's. By combining this way of looking at the issue with the calmness of your mind, the cleanliness of your de-muddled frequency, the guidance of your subconscious, and compete control over the meditative state, you will begin to discover solutions to the problem you have put forth in this courtroom.

When you are ready to exit the meditation, it's important to do so gradually, at least from my preference. I like to think of it as respecting the place that gave you peace by not just busting out the exit door and slamming it behind you. Do a countdown from ten to one or visualize closing one virtual door after another as you leave, with each door bringing you back to full consciousness. All the ambient noise, becoming louder and louder as you make your exit, your muscles start to wake-up, your physical senses coming back from their nap. By waking gently, you are also bringing the world you have discovered within you to the present. Whatever solution you have found in it, whatever message you have received, will still be with you as clear as it was when you were in full meditation. What you do with this information now is totally up to you.

Amazing, isn't it? That was all you! Just like riding a bicycle, you'll get used to the motions and become better at it. During your first several meditations, you will notice that you will rely less and less of the technique of getting into *the zone* and the process will be smooth. A seasoned meditator will be able to instantly quiet his or her mind with ease. A master will be able to meditate regardless of the distraction around him or her.

But what did we just do, exactly? What was the expected outcome out of all this? If you never felt that *ethereal* quality after closing your eyes and focusing on your inner-self during the exercise, then you are likely still glued to the awake version of yourself and not quite able to let go. Perhaps you're afraid of what could happen if you did let go or you have doubts that you carried with you. Maybe you didn't have the right environment to start the exercise to begin with or something distracted you during the process. Whatever the reason may be, just give it another try. I know you can do it! You, my friend, are far more powerful than you think. You are limitless and never bound by anything other than the limits you impose upon yourself (the same goes for practical day-to-day application).

If you, however, felt a sense of enlightenment, calmness that resonated even after you came back from the exercise, or just an all-around good feeling, then you're on to something! With enough practice, that feeling you achieved can expand and become your new *mental retreat*—a place exclusive to you for refuge, to obtain focus, to evolve. A place to cocoon the best version of yourself as it's going through metamorphosis. A state of being to suppress or deflect all the cognitive noise and filter your method of thinking. If you master the art of meditation, you will see that wherever you are, whether you're at work, at school, dinner with your friends, playing baseball, etc., you will find that ability to have an elevated sense of perception. Conversations flow easier and richer, business decisions are applied with immediate forethought, everything tastes better and your palette is more refined, you're able to hit that ball easier and with less distractions. The list goes on and on and on, the possibilities of what you can do have suddenly been enriched as if getting a boost.

With meditation, you have unlocked a tool that helps you fight against mundaneness and become extraordinary. It's a workshop of sorts as well that resides within you, your own mental office (or penthouse, or Fortress of Solitude, or *Shangri-La*, call it whatever you wish). That "inner space" is the incubator of the best ideas you can have and a place for it to expand. It's almost a dream-like state, and that is the beauty of it; you are disconnected from the usual senses that your focus becomes more tuned to what the subconscious thinks of and feels, therefore giving clarity to the truth that tends to get buried deep beneath. That space is the realm of your alter ego and where it can freely make decisions and, believe it, the conduit between you and the universe—a living gateway between you and God. The canvas of your greatest version ready to be drawn and painted, and you just discovered the paintbrush! Lucky you.

If my tone of subtle excitement doesn't get you thinking how significantly high the ceiling of possibilities has become, then think of the fact that you have discovered a place where there is complete freedom of thinking. When I say possibilities, I refer to the extent of how much you can visualize, imagine, and plan in this environment. It is important that you can think freely during meditation because that is your *castle keep*—the last place of refuge where nothing should be filtered, and it is also among your strongest tools when it comes to positive development in your life. It does not mean to just let your mind run amuck while you're in that state because in doing so, you will only get lost easily; your mind going in all sorts of uncontrolled directions, and there will be little positive point to meditating than just a way of random imagining. You must guide yourself to the state of calmness, learn to isolate and control, observe and react in a soothing manner, set your focus in order without being militant, and just listen. Feel—be at peace with yourself and the energy that surrounds you. Remember that the energy that flows thorough you is the same one that creates worlds. That same energy that can make manifest and instruct your ideas into existence is part of you and is present during meditation when you have the cleanest frequency to connect with it. So then, I ask, "What *do* you do with such an insurmountable presence?"

You make friends with it. You show your resolve when you're in it. You make yourself become familiar and at home with it and with nothing to hide.

In the present, where much of our attention is shifted towards the practical, we usually disregard our potential abilities in exchange for the situation we have to exist in. Meaning, the daily tasks we do such as work, sleep, eat, read the newspaper, drive to work, go to school, always set the rules for how we get to be successful around them. When we work, we have to ensure that our tasks are done, and we do them well. The reward in doing so is continued work, hence the money that comes to you, hence the ability for you to trade the money for life-support or desired items. Otherwise, we expect the outcome to have no job, no money, no means of living. When we don't get enough sleep, you know what happens. Energy goes down, productivity goes down, focus goes out the window. When we invest our time and effort on a practical process where we know there are repercussions for not doing so, it forces us to do it and live by its rules. I'm not asking for anarchy here and completely disregard these nor trade it for meditation, I'm saying there is a way to enhance yourself to take advantage of those processes and get the most out of them with minimal effort. There is a way to make your *practical daily living* work for you instead of wear you down. Because we are so integrated to all the daily things we do, we have been taught from Day One, and we are fully aware of the repercussions of not properly doing it, it is understandable why we think of ourselves as simply being common and that we were put on earth mostly to *turn a wheel*, recharge, and keep doing so until we find success. My goal is not to take you away from what you love, but to tell you that you can do and receive so much more. Remember what I said—You are limitless in many ways than just the physical.

Scientifically, your fully-awake brain is not needed to control most of your body functions. We knew this since the beginning, maybe in elementary science class or it was just a given. I.e., you don't have to think to digest, perspire, regenerate new skin cells, pump your heart, and so on. But you can, however, alter the way they all function from a subconscious level. To dial this concept down, a person who is exposed in a high-stress environment tends to show signs of stress on the outside and inside. They may look tired, get fatigued easily, have headaches more frequent than the average person, lose appetite, etc. While a person exposed to a low or no-stress environment has better physical mechanics and visual attributes. What we keep inside eventually shows on the outside.

I remember being in a relationship where I was constantly berated, humiliated, and disrespected. Though I was in my late 20's at the time, the destructive factors I was exposed to from the relationship got me looking much older for my age than I do now. My cholesterol was high, BMI (Body Mass Index) was high, I'd sleep from being exhausted and not because I was sleepy, and my thought patterns were scrambled and there was no focus (which permeated to my work performance). It was clear that what was affecting me consciously affected my subconscious and my state of health. It was an absolute ratio of *garbage in; garbage out.*

After I got out of the relationship and started the healing process, I realized there was a lot of work to do with un-learning and re-learning what a true relationship should be. Even more so, sorting what I want to keep in my life and what I muster the strength to remove. There is mental chaos after getting out of a damaging relationship. The heartbreak can be unbearable to many, the stress, the tears, the broken memories, they all pile one on top of another. To some, a distraction in the form of immediately finding another person to have a relationship with is how they avoid the pain of the loss. To others, they divert their attention and energy to activities that dull the sensation or force it to feel something else. But few, in comparison, decide to embrace and accept it, muster the bravery out of the situation, let alone give themselves the right to have a lengthy amount of time to recuperate and gain perspective. It's not only something one would need for one's self, but if they truly had feelings for the other person, they would find a way to pause time. Otherwise, it may very well be like putting a lid on a boiling pot and delaying the inevitable, and though not immediately but perhaps eventually, the stress will hunt and reclaim you. It always does. I've been there many times.

If there was one thing I learned from the years during this relationship transition, it was that whatever I consistently reminded myself of became me. Looking at all the past photos of myself during the relationship with lifeless eyes, it was clear that the stress was becoming me. It was making itself manifest through appearance and how I talked and how I reacted to things.

So then, I thought, "What if it was the reverse? If a drug addict shows the symptoms of addiction on the outside and an angry person always looks unapproachable, what would a person who practices positivity look like on the outside?"

Hence, this has been my life-long experiment—to see what I look like by the time I retire. So far, I will tell you that the results have been as expected. I look and feel younger. In fact, I even look younger now than I was decades ago. The youthfulness, the vitality, the approachability, the confidence, they're all showing. Also, just as it is difficult to stop the momentum of an object that has been moving for a long time, it is also difficult to reverse positivity if it is practiced often. Meditation helps by helping reason with difficulties through clear thought process, humility trains you to be grateful for what you have and appreciate what you are receiving. Letting-go denies any negativity from coming back and reclaiming territory inside you.

There is no limit to how many tools and techniques you employ to fix one problem. Just as you may fix a shattered vase with a tube of glue, you can do an even better job by incorporating a spatula, a brush, and a pair of tweezers.

The same rule applies for problems that
get in the way of your thinking.

That's how it works—you use not just meditation to clear your mind and reverse ill effects, you employ other strategies that we've talked about in the previous chapters, the rest, we will talk about and explore more. When you've learned to quiet your mind, it becomes easy to turn a detrimental situation into a positive one. With the diversity of methods, you can make any process easier, whether it is recovery or awareness. With practice, you can make it permanent.

Setting time aside to meditate and even just recognizing calmness is important. As I mentioned before, prayer is a form of meditation. Make it a habit to even pray regularly, whether it is just a prayer to say "thank you," the rosary, or recite a prayer you've memorized while you walk. And just as you show your discipline towards yourself when you meditate, exercise reverence in your religious communication with God. You are, after all, part of something much bigger than you can comprehend. So, find time for it, practice it often, make a habit out of it. Eventually, that space of peace will expand. It will become bigger and bigger, and it will overflow to your normal awake daily life and in your routines. Imagine yourself in full control of your reactions, walking around with a heightened sense of being and awareness, able to predict, be several steps advanced in thinking against your former self. Limitless.

This has been a lot to take in. Give yourself some time to let things sink in and expand. If this concept was new to you, I hope you'll have the sense of adventure to see how it affects you. Ultimately, I believe you can go far beyond the examples I've given. Keep this process and other methods of your healing private while you are using them to heal; don't go around telling everyone yet that you've discovered a new technique on how to recover from your mental wounds. When you're ready, you'll know when to tell those who need to know. For now, master it and enjoy it. There is time.

Put a bookmark here and explore your new realm. Go ahead! You know how to get there now. I'll be here upon your return.

CHAPTER SEVEN

FINDING THE REAL YOU

Hello again!

It's the perfect salutation to yourself in continuation of this journey, and I may add, to whom I hope you find in this chapter.

If you were to travel back in time, say to a point back in your life where you were a person just earning your first wages, what advices would you tell your younger self? Hopefully, you wouldn't be mad at yourself for any mistakes or missed opportunities you may have missed along the journey from then to now. I'm sure there is a ton of information you could empower your younger self with—knowledge, secrets, cheat codes to being successful, cautionary events that you should've avoided, and such. The question however is, would your younger person fully understand what you are trying to say? Would your naive-in-comparison-self fully grasp the concepts of how much life can unfold before him or her? The answer is probably not. We learn so much along the way that there are times, even a few months of learning from an unforgettable event that can seem a lifetime. But perhaps if you were to generalize instead of being specific with the information you were to pass-on, basing the idea on behavior present between your version now to your earlier version, then maybe you'd get your point across. But then, you'd worry if your younger version knew exactly what to do with that information. The truth is, it is inevitable to learn all these lessons along the way with all the little bits and details it will reveal; it cannot simply be granted upon you immediately like a magic wand and presto—you just *happen* to know everything. No sir/ma'am, it *doesn't* work that way.

There have been so many times that I've wanted to go back in time and *rescue* my former self from mistakes that he would encounter. My statements would've probably started with, "If you only knew what was ahead of you…" or, "Believe me, you're going to want to invest on…" or, "You're wasting your effort, do this instead…." I would absolutely trust myself with my whole life, but part of me would still wonder why I chose to do it that way. Even when a server at a restaurant brings your food over to your table and says, "Please be careful, the plate is hot," you'd still want to know exactly how hot the plate is when your server walks away by inconspicuously placing your finger on the plate. See? It wasn't just you who did that.

But that's time traveling in the past. What about now? For those among us meager mortals who can't afford a time machine, we obviously can't turn back the clock and what's done is done. What we can do, however, is change the future, and you don't need a time machine for that. Thanks to *Captain Obvious*, we know that it's possible to change the future, but what Captain Obvious may have not told you is how. Changing your future takes a *tremendous* amount of commitment, changing some significant attitude, and re-programming of one's thinking. This includes coming into terms with the past, preventing them from affecting your future decisions especially when they manifest, and more importantly, planning beyond that— beyond whatever goals you have in mind. It's simple to say that you will change yourself in order to change the future, but you need to create a solid foundation for the new you. One that does not cave-in at the amount of pressure nor crumble at the sight of discouragement. A *stronger* you. A *better* you. A much *wiser and resilient* you.

There is no limit to re-inventing yourself. Once you plant a flag on a plateau of your development climb, you'll notice there's more levels to go and the climb seems endless. But that's just how it works and that's just the way it is. We think that our development is about reaching a goal and then riding it out until the end of our time. Not really. You can choose to stay in the level you've decided to set camp for a while, but you will realize that things get difficult as you stay on that level. Maybe not in the effort that you exert but on keeping that level the same. Because of factors such as age, resources, the people around you, you will be prompted to keep going to the next level whether it's just a few steps away or a day's climb. Though you'll see that as you do so and make the move, life is providing you with encouragement in its own way. Sometimes with challenges, sometimes with rewards, but it will keep the vertical open for you to accept any chance of advancement. Just like the universe and life, you are expected to constantly evolve. You don't just stagnate on one level and call it good, because everywhere around you constantly changes. The one who adapts to all this change is the one who survives.

Along the road to the various levels and versions of you in the future, there will be times that it appears you are taking a step back. I can almost guarantee that there will be a few of these happening. These setbacks can be in the form of a loss such as getting let go from a job, or losing a loved one, or getting your heart broken, or feeling the discouragement that this is all that you can achieve, and you can't see past the next month ahead. Whatever these may be, they are not there to prevent you from getting to where you need to be.

Life does not present challenges to test you; life is training you to overcome them. Every milestone, every setback you encounter in life—all of them are for your betterment.

Sometimes, the setback can get so unbearable that it seems impossible to recover. Still, even in the worst of situations, there is always—and I emphasize *always*—an opportunity. Your objective is to discover whatever opportunity hides behind any unfortunate event and use it to slingshot you to the opposing direction. The best outcome of any unfavorable situation is your discovery of its opposing effect. The determination you make will be rewarded with positive results. This has happened to me so many times now that I no longer fear difficulty, challenges, or misfortunes. You will, too. The destructive reactions that you would typically display in an adverse environment will no longer be the tool you use to react to it. You will no longer feed the drama, neither will you feed the sorrow, nor the anger. Instead, you will encourage the solution, dispel the unpleasant emotions, and positively affect even those around you. The more you encounter these challenges and overcome them, the more successes you can put under your belt. In turn, you can harness your energy from these past successes and use them as propelling factors. What was once thought of as a deterrent instead became a motivator.

Use the tools you've learned so far—*acceptance, patience, forgiveness, peace, focus, humility,* and *perspective*—learn to utilize all of them, not just one or two. By now, you already know when to use each tool, what they signify, what they eliminate, and what they reinforce. Keep this discipline and no weight stands a chance to draw you downward. So never be hesitant to constantly re-invigorate yourself over and over. By the time you've changed for the better, whatever detrimental emotion that tries to claim you will no longer recognize the original person it was trying to bite on. It's attachment and purpose on you will be futile.

Even the cells in our bodies have a routine date when they hit the reset button. It's a scientific fact that a majority of parts of our bodies renew themselves completely every seven to fifteen years. Some, like the lining of our stomachs, renew themselves every five days due to digestive wear and tear. Five days! Therefore, by average, a person is 99% physically different from himself or herself a decade ago. It does this to let go of parts of you that are—as morbid as it sounds—dying. I mean, think about it. You'd be a walking corpse if your body never went through this cycle and your life span would be no more than just a sliver in your generation's history.

Like I said in the beginning, everything has a cycle. You are as connected to the cycle of life and the universe with your mere existence in more ways than just the metaphysical. Everything represents itself in different levels and different scales, but with the same general principle. The idea that your body from a scientific viewpoint depends on the ability to let go, heal, and manifest new versions of itself should be a huge clue on how justifiable it is to let go and rebuild one's self. Granted that the body does not lose its genetic traits (i.e. despite our ten-year-average renewal process, we still look similar, have the same hair color, blood type, and so on), the idea of re-inventing does not mean to start from scratch and build a completely different person, ideology, behavior, character, and all. We can't start from scratch; your body and soul are what you were given from the *get-go* and you are expected to use them as the proverbial *sand lot* for building new sand castles; new versions of yourself.

Just like any evolutionary cycle, the renewal process takes time. Time takes patience. Patience takes understanding and wisdom. Everything takes time. How you perceive time is a different story, and one that we will be discussing a bit in a future chapter. What this renewal process really is, is yet another series of opportunities to evolve and reinforce from the cornerstone foundations to the smallest details of your being. It's a chance you give yourself and one that life ultimately tells you that you have the right to do so. It is a God-given privilege to be able to self-improve.

Make a *renewal mantra*; a thought you play back during the day, especially when the day gets challenging. Take a walk and say it in your mind or audibly. Personally, I find that repeating this habit late afternoons after work not only resets me but gets my head out of the *work hole* where the only thing I can think of during the day are my day's objectives. I'll share with you my mantra as I walk. This is roughly along the lines of what I think of subliminally:

> *I am entitled to evolve just as everything around me evolves, therefore I take that opportunity and adapt.*

> *I am part of an ecosystem much bigger than what I can perceive yet I am an extension of the same energy that flows in it. I learn something every day.*

> *Today, I learned [insert something significant you learned here] and that gives me yet another item I can put in my mental book of wisdom. I can use this to improve and to improve the system around me.*

> *Any idea I create is possible, and there will always be guidance around me as I attempt to make it manifest.*

> *I am not bound by my daily routine. Though my daily routine is a*

necessity, it is what supports me, my future, my family. I do not live for my job, nor do I live for school. My job is here to sustain me, my education is there to enrich my future self. It is my passion within what I work for or what I learn the true reward of my efforts.

Just like today, tomorrow will be another day filled with opportunities. They will either come to me or I will find them and decide what to do with them as they come.

I will always be better than the person I was, and I will look forward to that person tomorrow.

Life will always guide me and will find a way for me. It is never always a straight line but there is a path and I am grateful for having that path.

I can change for the better and I can change what is around me for the better. There is no limit to how many chances I take to do so.

It's a rough sketch, really. Of course, you can create your own based on your perspective. You'll notice a bit of self-empowerment in the statements, and there is that outward perspective again, the letting-go, the sense of forgiveness. Your mantra will change over time as you discover more and more about yourself and your relationship with your guiding force. There is abundance in renewing and there is strength in renewing. You will realize that the limits you impose on yourself or that others set on you can be surpassed. You are a powerful being, capable of amazing achievement. When life hits you, you hit back hard, and the universe will always have your back.

Be humble with your renewals. You can think in a grand scale but remember that you are part of a much larger scheme than you can comprehend. Our arrogance is what gets us in trouble thinking that we know everything while our ignorance is what limits our knowing.

Especially for those of us working in an office or at school for most of the day, we can develop those work goggles and only see things from the perspective of our jobs or education. And it's true that every time we make something a habit, whether it is good or bad, will eventually make us think parallel to it. It becomes difficult to see the thousand-foot birds eye view when we are deep in the trenches. This is why not only taking breaks are important but so are vacations. They give you a chance to reset and reposition your thoughts on the matter so that when you take yet another deep breath and dive deep into the daily, you bring with you a refreshed thought pattern and a means to not feel so "stuck" with the card you've been dealt with.

Let me give you an example of how this renewal process can benefit you, and let's do a typical scenario for someone in the working class: Let's say that there is at least one person at your job who makes life difficult for you. Perhaps that one person just rubs you the wrong way somehow and undermines your contributions or downplays your role. Maybe not intentionally, though let's say that it was to assert superiority. The worst thing you can do is absolutely nothing and present your same self to that person every time you meet. But what if you were to present a different version of you? I'm not asking to take on a completely different persona or go full-blown extreme opposite in character, but a version of you more confident than before and calmer about the situation. I'm certain the person who was giving you a difficult time will notice that he or she is talking to someone now with a different reactive and thinking approach. If they're smart, they'll notice the subtlety in change and may even take some small corrective actions to adapt their approach to you. Little by little, they begin to adjust because the same avenue of reaction that they are used to from you no longer exists or doesn't go that far down the road. The person is forced to try a different approach. And, taking into consideration that you have a variance in your attitude in front of that person, you may also no longer need to feel threatened or disturbed when you meet him or her.

Bottom-line, renew as *often* as you need. Re-evaluate yourself constantly and groom your inner habits and thinking so that it's always easy to find parts that require maintenance. Get to know yourself very well inside and out. Invest on that knowledge and skill especially when a lot of our attention is misdirected away from our self-improvement in this lifetime. Reflect inward when you meditate; be mindful of your thoughts when you process them and listen for that "how does that make you feel when you think about it?" aspect. Renewing allows you to not only refine your future self, but it also does one other thing—allow the process of finding *the real you.*

Who is the real you? Who is the real [*insert your name here*]? This is a rarely asked question and one that few people don't really know how to answer. Most of the response to this question revolves around the background that we are exposed to. Our environment plays such a huge part of our life that it ultimately shapes us, and we know that if we try to go against that environment that gives us an advantage (in our own individual definitions), it may no longer support the advantage we seek. Say, if a young person finds his or her popularity on social media to be advantageous to their self-approval, they will keep at it while it still serves that purpose. We're always looking for ways to connect to our own "environment"—the beliefs we're taught, the trends we keep track of, the influence we receive from friends and family, the success we see in others we desire, and so on.

If a man loves to play the piano and is very adept at it, that man may have embraced an upbringing that included piano and all the fun that he had around it. As he grows older, the thrill and fun take a back seat and it just becomes second nature to the man. It becomes a predominant skill and honed which only keeps encouraging him. Should playing the piano be taken away from him, he looks for it, and may even yearn for it because it has already been a deep-rooted part of him. His heart is in it, his soul bound to it. It is an extension of him. Likewise, if a man has grown up to hate and criticize, he will know nothing but spread it as it will have become an extension of himself. He, too, will make it a part of him and it will become second nature to mudsling or throw careless judgement around. It is the environment and all the little nuances in it that make us and define us. Our interpretation of them is ultimately what leads to the generalization of who we are.

But what if we get down to the core? What if we strip away all the environmental influences that make us who we are, who will we see? This is a tough question. We never strip our identity by peeling the layers of influences. Remember, however, that you can be the person who plays piano and you can also be the same person who loves to criticize. You can have twins who grow up in the exact same household, go to the same school, attend the same classes, have the same friends, play at the same time, but they can still be independent of their choices and can grow up as two completely different people. The real question then becomes, "Who are you who have made yourself to be?"

Here's what we're going to do—we're going to go take a *visit* to your core. We're going to try and find out who the real *you* is. There will be no tests, just some visualization and honest intellect. We'll need to get there and find that person so that you know exactly who you are and who you're trying to rebuild and reset all the time. If you know yourself, then you know what makes you tick, where you can find the bad traits that live inside you, what direction you're really meant to go in this life, and you know how to build the best version of yourself in this lifetime.

Start with a clear mind, no distractions, and start peeling back the armor, the layers of your history. Think and answer quietly these questions and take your time to think of them before moving on to the next question.

If you are a working professional, what would you have been if you didn't take the job you're doing at this moment? Would you have done something different? If you are still in college, what if you couldn't pursue the degree you're attaining now; what path would you have chosen? What do you see yourself as? Can you visualize that person and his or her interests?

What would a conversation with that person be like if you met face-to-face with him or her now? Would you both still share the same interests and still be able to talk on the same level?

Would you be kind or critical to that person? If that person stayed on the alternate course, different from the path you currently chose, what kind of encouragement would you give him/her that would help in their future?

When you traveled back in time and saw your version as a child, would you introduce yourself or would you be completely invisible and observant? Would you emphasize your protective side, or would you allow your younger self to wander where the wind took him/her?

If you ever won something in your past—an achievement award, a place in a talent show, a friendship, etc., set them aside. If they never happened, would you be any different than who you are today? Would you rate yourself better? Worse? The same?

If you revisited a scene in your past that left you a scar or a grudge, would your attitude today be any different than if you never experienced it?

Name characteristics about you that you value; not material things that define you nor anything to do with physical attributes, but qualities about you that can stand the test of time for years to come. How did you allow them to integrate into your life? Do you value them more for what they give back to you or do you value them for what they offer to others?

If you had the chance to achieve a life-long goal right at this very moment, a goal that you would consider your "holy grail," the apex of what you strive for, what would you do? What would you change in your life and what would you keep?

Would you conspire to gain an advantage that puts you ahead of your schedule towards a life achievement? Would you rather be honest and mindful of who gets hurt along the way?

Do you plan and measure carefully before executing a plan? Or are you more comfortable in launching a plan with less scrutiny but course-correcting during its execution?

Where do you find peace? How do you define peace? Can you carry that peace in your mind or do you have to be somewhere to experience it?

Would you be comfortable just being by yourself or would you have a yearning for companionship? How do you define "self-dependence?"

Take as much time as you need to reflect on these questions. Take a comfortable walk by yourself or find yourself a peaceful corner to reflect. Start questioning yourself as if you're conducting an interview. Ask other things, personal things, things that you rarely talk about, inquiries about your upbringing and beliefs. Though you may already know the answer deep inside, you may sometimes be surprised at how you respond to them.

> *Be completely honest with yourself.*
> *Whatever it is you do in life, never under*
> *any circumstances adopt a deceptive*
> *principle. If you cannot be honest with*
> *yourself, you cannot achieve absolution,*
> *and your path will often revert.*

In other words, "Don't ever *B.S.* yourself." You are the only person who knows your own *Fact or Crap* game and if you try to convince yourself of a belief you know deep down is contradictory to your practical being, then you will only shoot yourself in the foot. Sometimes, accepting an honest fact is a difficult thing to swallow. That's why when we give ourselves a taste of our own medicine whether it's advice, criticism, self-control, it often tastes bad. We're not supposed to sugar-coat our own resolution. We can be direct with them, but we don't have to be harsh either.

If you have gotten to the deepest part of you after asking all these questions, who have you discovered is your core? Who is this individual piloting this mass of flesh called a body?

Your core is the most innocent, most vulnerable coordinator of your entire character since Day One of your awareness. If you find your core, you also find the path to understanding your purpose in life. Your core—the *realest* representation of you—is the purest definition of your individuality as a human being that hides behind the guise of an angry person to protect itself or the carefree boisterous person it likes everyone else to think. It is the one who sets the spark to your deepest desires, the dreamer who gazes at the stars, and the inner voice who whispers gently in your thoughts every day. It is the captain of your soul, protected and buried underneath layer after layer of years of restraint and refinement. It is the one whose initial actions are passed through your various levels of personal lessons and influences and presented on the surface as *character*. It is unequivocally the very first version of you, and it is this element who the universe has been trying to communicate with every day and who God hopes will notice all the positive encouragement he has been showing.

"Look around you! *Wake up*," life says to it constantly. "Look at all the beauty and opportunities I am showing you. *Please*, notice them! I believe in you. You can do great things and you are limitless for you are part of me, and I am part of you."

Have you learned so much about yourself by now? Were you able to identify the most vulnerable parts of your ego? Were you able to find the root causes of your behaviors? Did you discover how different you are now than you were back then? It's hard to let-go of old habits, we have a propensity to be hoarders of emotions and pile-on attitude and opinions we've gathered throughout the years. It's human nature to remember, that's how we can gauge where we're going or how far we've gone, yet if we've strayed so far away from the root of our being, we tend to forget who we are, and that gives room to making the same mistakes repeatedly or wonder why we can't succeed in doing something. Because you will be so familiar with yourself, you will know immediately whether you're making a good decision or a bad one in every logic that comes your way. You will be able to see past the emotions and have a clearer view of situations and problems. You will instantly know what makes you happy, what gives you the best satisfaction, and identify whether a trait is advantageous or detrimental in the long run. You can rely on your own when facing something alone and know better what to do. Self-discovery is amazing.

Never feel weird about observing yourself from the third perspective. 99.9% of our lives, we see things and make decisions from what we see in the first person. We're the pilot, we're the captain. We very rarely, if never, drive a car with our head outside the window. I wouldn't recommend it, but if you ever did it in a safe and low-speed situation, you'll notice just how odd yet amusing it feels because there's something you learn from it. You learn when you drive like that how much input the steering wheel has on the front tires when you pull it a certain amount because you see it as it happens. You know how much noise insulation is inside the cabin based on how audible the ambient noise is with your head outside compared to inside. You see exactly where the rubber hits the road and how much of the small deviances of the road surface get translated to your fingers through the steering column. Even if you happen to stop next to a building with a glass window, you can't help but look at your reflection and see not just yourself inside of your car but including the whole car itself. Why does it feel different suddenly sitting on the passenger side of your own car that you've always been driving?

Aside from knowing your history and interrogating yourself, being familiar with your core is much like seeing things from a different perspective. You see the real you—where you begin and where you end, and you get a good view of your preferences, your capabilities, and your level of awareness. Hence, whenever you press that *reset button*, you know what level to restart from and you don't overdo the reversion.

Many people find it difficult not only to renew but they also refuse to see themselves from another perspective other than from behind their own eyes. Maybe they're afraid of what they would see, who knows? Perhaps ignorance to them is bliss? Or perhaps they just don't know how.

…But you do! Remember as you put your suit of armor back on, your traits, strengths, even fears, you can always choose which parts you want to keep, and which ones you can let go.

Take some time to reflect on this chapter. There is no set standard on how much time you need nor amount of questions to reach your core. Only that it's there for you to get familiar with.

Once you do, rebuild...

Reset...

Redefine...

Relearn.

CHAPTER EIGHT

THE POWER OF BELIEF

This is the point in our journey where we begin to learn how to raise our heads up. This is the point when we have accepted the existence of our inner being and acquired the knowledge of a peaceful state that can open our core to endless possibilities. It's inevitable to think that all of that we've learned is not just purely coincidental. We know that we have learned immeasurable lessons over the years and that we've travelled so far, yet we also know that the entire collective album of what we've learned before starting this book is just one side of us. Deeper down, there is an intrinsic wonder: "What else is there for us?" and, "How can we possibly consider ourselves capable of greatness, if not more than the person we are today?"

Although your core is *extremely* vulnerable, it is connected to something far *greater* than we can imagine. It is connected to the source of all creation and it serves as a conduit to the same energy that creates worlds. Your very own factory of imagination is a world for it is a product of your thought orchestrated by what you currently know, anticipate, and assume.

When you imagine something, you are directing a play in your head. You become a scriptwriter, a composer, a strategist. Imagination is what allowed humanity to achieve flight and traverse continents. It toppled the first sequential domino of occurrences that gave rise to many innovations and historic events. The crime of this century is that it has been forged in our heads from when we were little that imagination is nothing more than a thought that never goes outside the boundaries of our head. We've been taught to believe that imagination is insignificant and that it carries little weight to an accomplishment versus the physicality of doing something. In reality, it is the genesis.

Can you imagine peace? Of course, you can. You just did when you meditated in an earlier chapter. Can you make manifest peace? Of course, you can. You just did after you came out of meditation. Wasn't that then a product of your thoughts? Of your imagination? Rather contradictory with the lesson you learned since kindergarten, isn't it?

This is exactly what an open mind can do to you—allow you to explore past the calculated boundaries set upon you by others such as your teacher or your family. I know they meant well, it's not their fault. They didn't intentionally misguide you, but their definition of imagination, belief, and the part you play with the universe is not something that has stemmed from their own self-discovery. They too, learned it from others and just passed-on this lesson, probably even added their own twist to it. This is the reason why it was necessary to learn how to let go and have the guts to relearn something that has been pre-programmed inside us. We are here to create a new version of ourselves; a better version, and we sure as heck won't surrender to the notion of *"it's just the way we were taught in the beginning."*

Since you started reading this book, we've been pioneering a new you and getting you to think outside the box—*way* outside the box, to a state where the richness of your mind really thrives. We are creators of our world, the environment around us, and we are entitled to make decisions that would be beneficial and advantageous to us which we aim to ultimately lead to the achievements we desire. We cannot be one to receive greatness if we do not believe that we can accomplish great things. Neither are we able to hear the truth from our own voices from a character molded by others.

Simply put, we can create and do, and it is only up to our own definition of limits how much of it we are able to achieve.

> *You are an incredible being capable of immeasurable achievement. The only limit is you.*

Take for example, a young girl who has no knowledge of what is beyond the town she grew up in. Over time, she reads many things about faraway places and hears stories of friends who have traveled far. She therefore can only assume what living outside her town must be like. When one day, she finally gets a chance to visit a foreign country and studies abroad. At that point, she can no longer unlearn; she knows what living in a completely different environment is like, and now she has a comparison and a choice. Her mind is aware of the new life and the new possibilities. She can judge for herself whether what she learned from living afar is something beneficial to her or something whose knowledge she can bring back to her town. Once you make the jump to see what is beyond your way of thinking, there is no turning back. It feels like you've grown.

The same can be said with believing. Believing is a key ingredient to many positive outcomes because it attracts opportunities and successes towards you. There are two ways to attract them—believing and expecting. One comes from within and the other comes from outside. But what is the act of believing?

Believing is a committed acknowledgement of a state of existence. Either you believe, or you don't, and whatever is in the middle are just different levels of doubt. It's not until you remove the last doubt when you are in the absolute state of believing. Belief also requires being resolute regardless of proof or nature towards what you believe in. You can believe in something positive and you can certainly believe in something negative. You can believe that something exists or that something doesn't. Whatever it may be, it is an unwavering direction.

Belief can also be used as an encouragement. If you've ever had someone tell you that *they believe in you*, it is a vote of confidence towards your abilities. If they truly meant what they said, they are loyal to the knowledge that you will succeed, and the proper way to honor the feedback is by removing any doubt. Would you ever rely on someone who doesn't believe in your abilities? Of course, you wouldn't! Then neither should you doubt yourself with your own abilities. Otherwise, it's kind of mutiny if you think about it. Your own crew must trust you, your inner being must be at peace and accordance with what you focus on. Therefore, if I told you that you were able to achieve immeasurable successes, would you doubt me simply because you cannot agree with that? If so, then you will have not learned anything at this point and you may as well be part of the statistic. But I don't believe that. I am positive that once you grasp the teachings in this journey, you will surpass your own expectations and you will not only refuse to revert to your previous self, but you will have such an unstoppable drive that whatever you put your imagination on, the wisdom and guidance of the universe will team-up with you.

As you can see, believing is some serious business. You can imagine all you want, but if you never believed in your imagination, nothing would ever come to fruition and nothing would escape the confines of your mind. The belief system is also not just something of your own doing; it's a mutual relationship. The person who believes is relying on the reciprocal action he or she believes in for the circuit to become complete. When you believe in something, you rely on the universe to help you plan your goals accordingly. Provided that your faith is strong in something you may not physically see, you are in expectation that the universe (or God) will provide you with a path towards your goal. Sometimes, your goals adjust and changes or evolves, and the universe adjusts accordingly. Since the universe is a living being, it too adjusts and evolves. Even its plans on your goals evolve and you may find it telling you, "I have something better planned, you're going to like it for sure, but first, let's go this way…." But more on that later. Your belief must be mutual, plain and simple.

"If I, the *Universe*, believes in you, so should you believe in me," is what it's saying. "If I show you a path towards the success you desire, so should you show a path towards the faith you have on me. We are one—*you* are part of *me* and *I* am part of *you*. If one of us does not trust the other, there is misalignment and we will not see eye-to-eye."

The supporting pillars of belief are *faith* and *trust*. If you trusted your life to a surgeon, you believe that the surgeon can fix the infirmity and whatever physical vulnerabilities you have. To trust something or someone means that you are willingly offering an unconditional connection to something that exists. Trust is an acknowledging positive response to the connection towards the existence of, or product of, an event, idea, or being.

Faith on the other hand, is an investment in that trust and whatever outcome it has, most especially if it is unknown. Faith and trust are interchangeable to many, but faith is more powerful in the sense that it does not require proof. Faith is where you are given the mere understanding of something and commit to acknowledging its existence. It may sound illogical, but unless you don't know how devoted religious fanatics can be, it's hard to understand. Faith is reserved for ideas and beings who are powerful enough to require no proof whatsoever. Our faith in God, our faith in the existence of a much higher absolute order, our faith that life will go on. And there's also another thing, you hardly or never hear anyone use the word "faith" in a negative connotation, have you noticed?

If the direction of the verb is directed towards you, it also changes the tone. For example, if someone said, "I trust that you will win," it would carry a different feeling than the same person saying, "I have faith that you will win."

"He trusts me" versus, "He has faith in me." It's not one better than the other, it's just different yet they're connected and relatable. Both are ambassadors of believing.

People have different levels when it comes to believing. Some believe by seeing, others by seeing and touching, others by seeing, touching, and experiencing. During your young upbringing, you often learned (or were tricked) by investing in a statement an adult claimed.

"The moon is made of cheese," for example. Do you believe it? Have you been to the moon as proof? If no, then how do you factor in the condition that it isn't? How do you know if the close-up photos of the surface of the moon resemble parmesan and not rock?

We can go on and on scrutinizing the various ways we can define faith, trust, and believing. But where does *"hope"* come in?

Hope is a coin toss. Hope is wishful thinking. Hope is a request to materialize instead of a command to make manifest. Hope is not a bad thing, hope is what sparks the birth of positive encouragement and action, but it is not the switch that rallies our spirits nor is it the horn that bellows when it is time to fight. Hope is wishing that you will see your soul mate again someday, and belief is knowing that the story is never over.

Believe in yourself. *Invest* in your future successes. Bet on your abilities that they will carry you through. If roles were reversed and you were the universe, the guiding power, even God himself, the absolute power in heaven, how would you feel if you tried to encourage one of your creations to pursue and live the best life possible, yet it only gave minimal effort, enough to just get by? You forged the ultimate instrument of power on Earth and all it aspires to be is a glorified paperweight on somebody's desk. No, this is certainly not us.

Here then, is the new lesson we should learn; the lesson that should've been taught to us from Day One of our realization towards our discovery of the world around us, and one that should be taught today:

"To believe is to achieve. You have the power within you, literally within you, to direct your future to the best possible version of yourself and affect outcomes along the way for as long as you believe. Believe that there is a higher power always looking over us and that it is not just an invisible wish for guidance. We live amidst a fully-functioning relationship with the world, with God, with the universe, and even with time. Merely working hard repeatedly is not the best way to success. You must never make haste where you invest your beliefs in and which part of you that defines it. We are makers, creators, a manifestation that can make manifest, and the pawn in the game of Life that Life wants to see win.

The time it takes for success to mature is less relevant to us and is more the business of the guiding force we learn to appreciate and have faith in every day. We are the doers of the inspire-filled imagination we produce. We are the endpoints of the creative energy that flows all around us and the conduit of creative elements such as love, selflessness, tolerance, harmony, understanding, and patience. We are more than able to make a difference in this lifetime whether it is to ourselves, the people around us, even beyond the limits of what we can see.

Time is not our enemy, it is our catalyst and the road that takes us to places and events. Our existence is to provide the fulfilment of our dreams through the encouragement, blessings, and guidance that the universe gives us at a constant basis. The bearing of our failures should only impact the adjustments and slight deviations we do to make ourselves better, never as a crutch for self-vindication towards self-righteousness.

We all have a purpose that we serve in this life, the next life, or the generations that follow us. The more you believe in your cause, the more the universe will see your commitment and it too will commit to your cause. You will see signs along the way, signs you've never seen before but encourage you and continuously represent hints and clues as to what should be your next step in your commitment. You are part of the endless cycle of creation, recreation, and evolution that represents itself in so many levels.

The mind may play tricks, but the heart never lies so follow your heart and allow it to have a healthy relationship with your mind and its intent. Use your creative senses not to tug on the leash, but to guide yourself smoothly and kindly.

Finally, if you can never muster the belief that the universe is here for you, then at the very least, believe in yourself. Happiness is born from within by what we emit and less from what we receive. The external entities that make us happy such as the approval we get from friends, the joy of a goal's benefits, or the care of a partner in life, is the reflection of our response to them. Ultimately, it is us who makes us happy and entitled to believe what we choose to believe—not our parents, not our coaches, not our teachers, not our best friends. Just us."

The only entity responsible for our own happiness is us.

Before we embark on another climb up the wall of mindfulness and closer to the launchpad, let's be aware of where we currently stand. You know that believing will empower you and will be the inner driving force of your manifestations for your goals. You know that it had been an untapped ability you've possessed all this time just screaming to be untethered because it believes it will not only get you from Point A to Point B in the most effective way, but in the most life-enhancing, most meaningful way as well. Use it in the following chapters. Hold on to it. In your mental toolbox, belief ranks as the most powerful tool. It is because of belief how this book came to be and how I was able to fill its pages with thoughts somehow channeled to my fingertips with relative ease and insight from some world-creating source. I and the product that is this very book you read are proof that believing will initiate the handshake between you and the source of all life, and it will take you by the hand and lead you to endless amazing adventures and prosperity. You've struggled all your life to understand your purpose and to discover your fullest potential. All you had to do was believe.

The energy you emit when you become positive can be *contagious*. Take this simple experiment and see for yourself: When you are at a supermarket or just walking at a park, anywhere where you will run into people that will notice your presence, smile a bit. Not a huge, crazy, teeth baring grin, but just a subtle *Mona Lisa* smile. As you walk and pass people, you will notice—even without making any eye contact—that they too will smile! Perhaps even bigger than yours, sometimes they will make eye contact, sometimes they will just smile. Your smile disarms them and gets them to subliminally think that you are not of any threat. But it is a reaction, and the same thing happens when it comes to you and the universe.

When you feel positive and you emit positivity, as crazy as it may sound, the universe will respond back and be attracted to you and pay more attention to you. If you demonstrated self-confidence, believed, and had the personality of one who is at peace, the universe *will* respond. Feel depressed, angry, and the universe will respond to it as well with even more gloom and provocation. Simply put, you reap what you sow, what goes around comes around, garbage in—garbage out, you attract what you become, and you receive more of what you reflect outward. In other words, positive thoughts attract positive thoughts. All the universe does is say, "Yes." It doesn't pity you for it knows you are able. Its nature is to nurture and emphasize you, not reverse your feelings.

"I feel great!"
"Yes, you do!"

"Cotigo, ergo sum." ("I think, therefore I am.")
"Quidem, tu es." ("Indeed, you are.")

"My life sucks."
"Agreed. It sure does."

You attract more of what you believe and become. Think of why positive people cannot be let down no matter the situation or why pessimistic people never seem to stop coming across something to complain about. An angry driver will always have people cut him off on the freeway. An impatient woman will always run out of time. Life will keep giving you, yes, but it will give you what you ask for and what you believe. It's not a metaphor; it literally *will* try and give you what you ask for. These include circumstances, not just reactions to your attitude from other people. So why not wish yourself and others well? Why not have faith in yourself? Why not send an invitation to the universe to believe with you by showing examples?

You were designed based on your own personal interests, your conceived dreams and imaginations, and your past and present help align you to your preconceived success.

I invite you to try it out. No one can ever fault you for wanting to feel positive about yourself and change your outlook in life. Isn't that what this journey is all about? This chapter may be eye-opening to some, and you may find conflicting signals from within arguing quietly about the proof of validity and thinking, "This is not what we were taught!" I know. *Tsk-tsk*, shameful. You could've gotten the cheat codes to life at an early stage, but *no*, people who didn't know how to truly believe went the hard way and passed on their map. There's a better way to seek fortune than just hunting and pecking. You have sponsorship with your positive actions and a corresponding law of reward. Just believe! It really *can* be that easy.

That next chapter will tie to this for sure. We will discover how you can tell if you are going the right direction and what kind of cues and clues life is sending you. But take a break, put a bookmark on this section before you proceed and reflect on this chapter. Your potential success relies on you unlearning the old logic and replacing it with this new one. You can still retain your values and your core beliefs, but you can also enhance and refine them at the same time. You can move mountains, my dear friend.

Believe it.

CHAPTER NINE

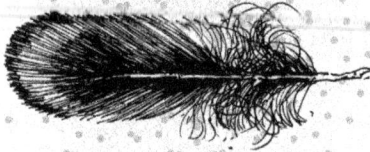

SIGNS OF THE TIMES

In an earlier chapter, we talked a great length about meditation and its ability to get you to clean the frequency and achieve focus. This was the method on how you gave clarity to your daily decisions and this was also the environment where you sent your intentions. By finding your core, you were able to know more of who you are as the requester and give more meaning to your goal, whether it is truly what you want, or if it was just to fill a void. You know how to wield the conductor baton of your life now and find alignment with yourself, the universe, and your objectives the proper way. Not that too long ago, we learned new formulas, new ideologies on your relationship with the forces that guide and encourage all of us. Even the patterns in the cycle of life are evident in our beliefs as we are constantly nurtured in a give-and-take relationship with the universe, the Creator, and with the power within us.

Now however, it's the universe's turn to reciprocate a response, and it will do it in its own special way. If you can zoom-out of the whole picture, you must realize that you are dealing with an entity that does not have any limitations whatsoever. You know that you cannot demand something from the universe nor force it do something. A fruit does not demand anything from the tree it came from.

Let's make one thing clear before we proceed:

You are not above the system, neither are you "the system." You are part of the system and the system wants you to be part of it. You are its physical extension, much like a limb or a branch. Be respectful and always know your place.

You have its attention though. A bravado attitude will never work because it can see through you and it's all too familiar with the core of whom it's talking to. Be vulnerable when you talk to the universe and feel vulnerable, it's okay. An honest relationship with the energy that creates worlds will honor you by fully-furnishing the home of your achievement. What's more, the undiluted feedback you give it will be its manner of response to you. In other words, "Toy with it, and it will toy with you because that is what you give it and it only agrees in return."

You can probably imagine what children can manifest because of the genuineness of their beliefs, granted they won't manifest the same desires you do at your age because they have different desires and limited exposure to the grand things in life. Still, their belief of acquiring something is strong compared to us for their thoughts are completely unfiltered and innocent. They know nothing of the complexity that adulthood introduces to one's life and they carry on knowing that they are always looked after and that someone will always tend to them when they fall or when they get hungry.

How do you make a proper request? The same way you would if you were standing in front of your creator— sincere, calm, accepting, and grateful. You are your creator's dearest friend, most trusted agent, and symbol of love. Return to the Creator what is rightfully the Creator's. State your requests clearly and cleanly. There is no need for theatrics or embellishments. Trust that your request's fulfillment is underway after you have presented it. Believe that the system is working and that it will need you to take action at the time it presents the opportunity to you. If you miss that opportunity, another one will be formulated so don't beat yourself up for any opportunity you may have missed.

"When one door closes, another opens," as the saying goes. Believe with child-like anticipation and expect with a mind open to all sorts of possibilities.

Be patient after you make your request. Put it in the queue of the universe managed by a timeline that is not for you to control. Do not spend all your energy finding the prize—trust that *it* will make its way to you. If you keep thinking of the absence of what you are trying to manifest, you will never get out of the loop of requesting. Trust that a *program* is already being developed for you and time of development is irrelevant. Should you feel any anxiety as a cause of waiting for whatever it is you are trying to manifest happen, learn to calm it through meditation. Remember that the enjoyment of your goal is not only the result of when it comes to fruition, but it's also the journey itself as you're getting there. You need to enjoy that journey—really savor it because it's the small details along the way that give your goal the most meaning. And it's not really your goal that defines you. The goal is the result of your efforts; it is a representation of your character's achievement, the icing on the cake, but it is not what gives you the rich substance of your composition. Nothing lasting and cherished ever comes from immediate gratification, and therefore the typical person's knowledge of time is limited to just a form of waiting instead of the amazing journey.

The path you take also becomes a user guide for when you take a similar one in the future, or if you plan to coach someone else with it. Getting to the next goals become easier and easier when you relish each journey and extract life-altering epiphanies along the way. Every story has a pattern in whose ending won't make sense until you see how the character got there. In a video gamer's terminology, "More XP to level-up."

Be careful trying to project too far into the future and anticipate the exact result you are going for in your journey. Expectations are tricky because they can create a feeling of disappointment if not fulfilled the way you envisioned it. Disappointment can turn into doubt, and doubt can fall into disbelief. Be open minded. Don't think that every journey is a straight path that takes you from beginning to end. There's lots of twists and turns, setbacks, and bonuses along the way, and it was designed that way to help us learn. The universe, with its infinite wisdom, will always know far better than us when it comes to the path we must take and the goal at the end. It will add or subtract elements from your journey if it sees it fit that you can have something better. Often, it's the path that takes a twist to an unexpected route. You may throw a fit, cry, or be angry at the change in the scenery along the way, but the universe will just sigh and raise its eyebrows at you, because you will eventually realize that what it was trying to do is provide you with a better alternative. Again, this is why you should never feel disappointed at events that happen whether they are favorable to you or unfavorable.

I once held a job role in the tech industry I absolutely loved only to be booted out after a year. It was what I referred to back then as "a dream job." It paid handsomely well and the large number of hours I would put into my projects was something I never got tired of. Often, I would work until the early morning but because I enjoyed it so much, I never minded at all. I had a lot of respect and recognition from my colleagues, but it just didn't last long enough, and I was forced out of the company.

"It was absolutely unfair," I protested, and I fought tooth and nail to try to get back in or justify the shortness of my employment, but it was not happening. But back to the day I got let go, I remember trudging back to my car, head hung low and all. I might as well have a rain cloud above my head. I could barely compose a thought and all I could feel was anger and bitterness. I pulled myself in and it took me several minutes before I could regain my motor skills. There was one part of it I clearly remember that will last me a lifetime, and it was more powerful than the negative emotions I held that day—the part where I surrendered.

"Show me the way, Lord. Just show me the way," I said. "I will follow."

Little did I know then that the course of events would take me to an even bigger success than if I had stayed with the company, and the success was worth far more than the financial rewards or any corporate gain. I would not be the far better man I am today if it wasn't for that kink in my journey, and if I was to be presented with a way to turn back the clock, I don't ever think I'd want to go back. What I have now is far greater wisdom more valuable than money. I can create my own fortune and I can achieve far more than my talents could've taken me. It may sound like a bluff or rhetoric to some, but this really is how I feel and how I wish everyone could as well. Had I stayed with that job, I'm very sure we would never be talking right now. Since then, I knew that everything that happens, favorable or unfavorable, is always for the betterment in some way, shape, or form that is far beyond what we can comprehend at the time.

"Always happens for a reason. *Always*," I often say. It's up to us to find out what that reason is. That is one of many facets the way the universe talks to us.

With every misfortune comes a packaged opportunity.

"...But through misfortune?"

No, not *always* through misfortune. Of course, I'm not saying that all misfortunes are a blessing in disguise, but there is always a developing opportunity to turn it around if we don't get stuck in it. There is most certainly always something we can learn from it and it's often something we never expect.

There are so many success stories floating around from leaders and entrepreneurs saying, "If it wasn't for [this problem], I wouldn't have done [this opportunity] and it wouldn't have taken me to [this level of success]." Quotes such as, "Rising from the ashes" or, "What doesn't kill you makes you stronger" are part of what this is.

First, it's the ability to move forward after a mishap, and second, it's the ability to find the opportunity to become better so the mishap never happens again or that we can find positive direction in our course away from it. In contrast, we also hear people brandish the *woe is me* or *my life sucks* attitude whether it's over a social media post or when asking for support from a friend. The people in your life who love and care for you will come to your aid, but it is ineffective to lead a cause when the underlying tone is one of hopelessness. Strategically, one should never use pity as a message to rally support unless it is pity you seek (misery loves company after all).

Success from a difficulty is the ability to move forward from that difficulty. Wallowing in it is no different than a car getting stuck in mud. It'll just get worse the longer you're there. The reason why inspiring stories such as the triumphant return of one who has come from battling a disease or the overcoming of an oppression stick with us so well is because of the message behind it. It is proof that it is possible to invert a detrimental situation and it is a *chalk one up* to the incorruptible spirit of humanity. It's what we want to be—triumphant and resilient.

What do signs of the universe's encouragement look or feel like then? Truthfully, it varies from person to person and the signs are all personalized. You may think, "There are over seven billion people in the planet and you're telling me each and every one of them has their own personal communication from the universe?"

Absolutely! And if so, are you *still* doubting? Just because we cannot fathom the diverseness and complexity of the universe does not mean we have to accept a simpler explanation. Our minds are simply not designed to cope with that complexity, but the fact is that since each one of us here on Earth has a distinct path in life, so are the signs that are given to us. It's as complex as a library filled with biographies for every living human. Yet to the Creator, it would be comparable to a pocket diary he carries every day.

As I said, the signs vary from a mix-up of physical manifestations, feelings, natural phenomena, sensory input, and everything in between. What you are most tuned in to, is where it manifests the most. The common denominator for all these signs across every human is the character of emotions felt. Earlier in this book, we talked about our interpretations of emotional stimulus. A looming cloud could appear ominous to some but comforting to others, for example, so there will never be a way to pinpoint exactly what signs are appropriate for you.

The signs find *you*, however. That is the inexplicable pattern that happens when you ask the universe for a favor. I can recall days when I would think of a specific thought and a person would just come up to me and utter something like, "Things happen for a reason," which was an example of an appropriate response to my thought at the time. Sometimes, it would come in the form of music in the background whilst waiting at the dentist's office. Sometimes, it's the way a wave crashes by my feet on the beach.

If you haven't gotten yourself to believe by now that the strangest things are often the ones we simply cannot comprehend, you may very well categorize this occurrence as *ridiculous* or *absurd. Comical* even. But if you do believe, with your newly-found wisdom which I know you have, you accept the fact that you have experienced your own signs one way or another. Even the sudden inexplicable surge of energy during an uphill run is enough to get your mind wondering where it came from.

Throw whatever is left of your old logic out the window, *dearest*, for it will only be a limiting factor to understanding your relationship with the universe. If you are fully committed to change, then you will experience change not through doubting but through faith. I will say it again—you are reading proof, line by line, of a manifestation in the form of this book and a translated relay of an ethereal source by an individual who only chose one day to surrender to God. I have no intention whatsoever of leading you astray and never force you to believe what I believe. Neither will I belittle your decision if you chose not to. I only wish for you to partake on what I experience for it is limitless potential and I believe we can discover it together. We are far past doubt. Let it go.

The signs are clearest when you are in alignment and at peace with yourself. Things will simply stand-out and will catch your attention even when you don't look for them. You will see them in every day normality such as encouraging turn of events that seem to *make way* for an opportunity. Patterns repeat such as numbers or experiences. To some gifted people, dreams are a direct line of communication when it comes to signs because it is when we have no way to exercise doubt. They can be subtle, or they can make your heart jump. The biggest frustration here is that it is impossible to point out exactly what you should be watching out for when listening or noticing these signs. This is the part of this book that I simply cannot explain, only that they appear when you have clarity and the absence of conflict in you.

But also, "Don't play too hard," as a friend told me once. When you attempt to lavish any sign that you encounter by over-defining it, then you will miss the point. Imagine someone telling you, "Hey, look! A shooting star," and you start to go ballistic asking yourself, *"What direction was it headed?"*

"Was that sort of towards my ex's old house so does that mean something?"

"Did the star have a shade of color that matches my favorite football team's jersey? Will that mean that they will win this season?"

"So, does it mean that it answered a 'yes' when it's going away from me or is that a 'yes' when it's going towards me?"

I think you get the idea. As I said, let them come to you. Allow them to flow into your life naturally. Seeking for them every time will not only exhaust you, but it will also render you numb from looking at every little thing as a sign. And don't think that you'll miss the signs if you don't look for them. They will keep repeating in many different but subtle ways. We won't have to worry about losing focus on just one thing, remember that the universe is highly advanced and adept at passing information to you. You don't have to take one sign as the *ultimate sign* unless it's considerably obvious, like the heavens unsealing, a beam of light shining on you, and you hear angels sing.

Humor aside, it almost never happens this way because if we experience signs in this manner, we will never want to listen to anything else but any sign with a similar intensity and we will keep looking for that same level of communication. Then, when we never find that enthralling modicum of a cosmic event, we'll just be disappointed for the rest of our lives. Do you get it now? The wisdom of the universe right there, in plain common sense. The universe doesn't want to disrupt your course drastically. It guides you gently instead of abruptly yanking on your bridal. It tells you where to go in subtle ways to not interfere with the natural course of life. It just comes easily and almost naturally that you may mistake it as something even you came up with. A thought would waft into your head and you would suddenly get an impulse to do something, or a tune in the background would remind you of an event associated with the feeling, and the feeling makes you take a certain course in a decision you were making that day. That kind of subtle. When you receive it and it feels like it's part of something normal and yet appropriate for the present, you'll know.

There's also another way life drops hints—it's via the changes in your attitude and how people act around you. For example, let's say your goal is to become a famous person someday, and you believe it to be true which starts the process of manifesting, your attitude becomes your barometer or the gauge you use to determine how much of change is happening. Then, you'll notice you start becoming more confident, words flow easier when you talk to someone, you almost sound as comfortable as a celebrity over dinner after receiving an award that night. You notice these changes, and consciously enough, they're not the usual *you* that you know. If you're relatively observant, you'll see the range of difference between your version before and the present and you realize that you *are* the sign.

From that point on, it's a domino effect: you start getting noticed by other people, your spouse or friend sees your changed positive attitude and they adjust accordingly to reciprocate that observation, your usual talks with your co-workers start to get more interesting and deeper, and so on. Your belief in yourself basically allowed the universe to easily inject that proverbial upgrade and your goal of being famous started to manifest through you instead of around you. Doesn't that just make you see this manifestation business a whole different way now? Amazing stuff not everyone would've thought of.

Sometimes, the signs become deeply-integrated into your daily routine that you never realize you're already experiencing it. If we took the previous example earlier about wanting to become famous, you may have gotten used to people treating you nicely that the change fades into the background and you just carry about your day thinking that life was good.

"The sun was always shining whenever I felt like it, there was always something great to look forward to especially on the weekends like some sort of social gathering that I really enjoyed," or the expectation of something great and positive was continuous. Speaking from personal experience, I seem to get this rather frequently.

No, not the part about being famous but getting so accustomed to the change that it just starts to feel *normal*, like the transition between *before and after* is so seamless. In this scenario, it's just best to go along with it and don't stop or change your attitude to question the change. It just *is*, and that's all you need to know. Keep calm and carry on, you know? If you ever catch yourself in that moment where you make that realization, just enjoy what's happening and keep doing what you're doing. It makes it easier for the universe to continue the positive program it has enrolled you in when you don't question it. If you fed your cat and it played with the food before eating it, you'd be a bit irritated.

"I gave you this and what are you doing with it? Stop it!"

There's also this thing called *contrast* and it's something you should allow to happen as you go through your transformation. Contrast can be in the form of things not happening the way you expected it to, or even situations happening against the direction you're wanting to go. It could be a setback, or it could be in the form of a failed attempt at doing something. If you remember earlier about opportunities and how they present themselves in many ways including unfavorable circumstances, there is opportunity in this one facet to learn. Contrast allows you to take corrective action because it is not headed towards the direction you want, and it is a required adjustment to steer you back to the right heading. Just like when you want to keep your pet from going into a certain room of your house, you put a block on that path to deter the animal from that area. Whether you see it as a challenge to overcome or as a full stop is totally up to you. You'll know either way whether you encounter the same exact block or a different one. And if you decided to plow through it and you weren't supposed to, I guarantee the universe will put another block, and another, until you never realized that you're slowly being pointed back to the right course again.

As you can see, the universe doesn't talk to us using words in a common human vocabulary. Its highly advanced language allows for the use of other methods of communication us humans were not designed or keen to utilize such as the emotions we commonly experience, interpretations of occurrences that we observe, the generalization of a grand situation, or the insignificance of a sudden reaction. Amidst all this, the focus is always going to be on us and we understand it by observation of patterns, intensity, timing, and the method that the universe uses to communicate. The book we write about our own personal interpretation to visions and signs is really for our eyes only, but the methods shared on how they are relayed to each one of us are common. We know what a sunset is. We know what a quiet breeze feels like. We are familiar with the beauty of the sun shining when it rains.

Always remember that manifestation develops naturally through a process of evolution versus immediate gratification. You cannot assume one sign as the only sign you will encounter along the way. There will be many, I promise you, and they will keep coming sometimes in the funniest moments. We're not supposed to understand how they got there, but only that they're there. And should you feel insecure about your interpretations thinking they're way off course, don't worry. The universe will teach you how to read and interpret them. You have this *amazing* relationship with it and it will teach you so many things you never knew were possible. The limits of what you can learn are immeasurable and yet it will keep inspiring you to explore more and more.

What a great relationship! The universe caring enough about you that it personalizes all communication with you and never runs out of stories to share with you. That's what makes you and I special, you see. The immeasurable differences we have with one another in this world, yet we all answer to one.

The next time you're outside, look around. Everything that you see can be used as a sign. So many varied ways of talking to you and so many situations you can find yourself communicating back and forth. I hope it's a great relief that because you believe in yourself and what you can accomplish, that you also have the privilege of being able to have an out-of-this-world conversation with a being far more immense than you. You are connected to that! All of that! *Wow!*

CHAPTER TEN

SPREADING YOUR WINGS

In springtime, a flower blooms to start the cycle of reproduction and to attract insects and other animals. It begins its journey from a bud making its way to full bloom, and it does so as it spans a length of time and caring. As it reaches maturity, it encourages the start of another cycle—one that is outside its own. Animals of sizes benefit from it, and that includes us, humans. They use flowers for food, to attract other creatures on the lower food chain, or decorate someone's home. It gives itself willingly to the greater good, for although that purpose is something it is not aware of, it is however designed for. To acknowledge that you are part of something bigger than yourself and everything you can contain in your vast knowledge is not only to willingly accept the potential of your existence and role in this life, but it is also to welcome the possibilities of where that can take you and who it can affect. Much like spreading your wings not only a preparative prelude to the act of flight, but symbolically a gesture of one who surrenders to one's purpose.

Someone dear to me once said, "You make the best version out of everything you have." And why not? What is there to gain from by objectively wearing something down? If you can improve on a system or something you possess, you enable it to last and evolve. A car, for instance, something many often regard as a utilitarian machine, will take you to places and adventures. If taken care of and reasonably maintained, it will serve you for as long as it is designed for. A relationship that fosters encouragement and stability will last the test of time given the reciprocal care, understanding, and love it deserves. Even talent that we already possess can take us to unexpected fortune as long as we encourage it to grow and expand. Much like what you invest on your own self, if applied with care and positive encouragement, it can serve you for as long as it takes, perhaps even beyond your expectations than a machine would, for any investment you put upon yourself is always a good investment.

This chapter is dedicated to you—our sons and daughters, our brothers and sisters, mothers and fathers, caretakers, adventurers, lovers of life, philanthropists, innovators, leaders, makers, dreamers, and everyone else in between. You are the future and the ones I look forward to seeing make the biggest splash in the river of life. I know you not in race nor gender nor religion, but that you are as every bit human as myself, capable of amazing feats, of what is seemingly impossible, even incredible. Your goal is to surpass yourself, not against one another.

You will go through difficulty. With difficulty, it surfaces an opportunity to improve. No matter how steep the wall that you must climb over to excel, always remember that you are *literally* a product of a higher cause and you have the given ability to challenge that difficulty and overcome it. The first battle always starts from within. Win it, and you will gain significant momentum to completely turn the situation around for your benefit rather than let it stop you. This requires you to remove all doubt. There is no room for doubt in belonging to a higher cause. The challenges will keep coming, and you will keep pressing on. Every win becomes a stepping stone, not always a trophy, and you use it to prove to yourself that you are more than capable. As I mentioned, Life will always have your back. All it wants you to do is remove fear and doubt. Trust it. Believe it!

As you go along the journey, you will encounter people and situations that will make you pause and think, "Am I going the right direction with this?" You will encounter plenty of them, I assure you, with varying levels of how much they change your *shoot-from-the-hip decisions* or even your entire life. One thing regardless of who you may meet in every journey:

"Always remember them for the good things they are."

Even the worst of people you know have characteristics you can admire. They may have the tenacity, they may confidently believe they are right with no regrets, or they may be a master at their trade. No matter how they appear offensive to you, there is something you can learn from them. Remember as much of the good as you can in others, and always look for those traits. Learn to *de-emphasize* the unfavorable things you find in them—most especially those who have wronged you. Although we do not praise them for those traits, and nobody will have a perfect record towards everyone, if the tables were turned and you were the object of offense, would you want to be remembered solely for all the mistakes you did? Would you be made as an example for other unfavorable traits and put in that category? Or would you rather have inspired someone of a trait that makes them want to follow that part of you despite how against they were towards your beliefs?

There is always good in people. Always.

You gain absolutely *nothing* by putting down someone else or looking down upon them, only that you have fallen into the trap of comparing yourself against them to which is not only petty, but you would have missed the whole point of belonging to a larger cause. You climb the hierarchy of status not by pulling someone down, but by raising yourself up. Again, it does not matter what level you perceive they are in whether it's above or below you. You will begin to compare to them, if so.

"So what if *he's* greedy? So what if *she's* so self-absorbed?" Everyone goes through their battle, you just never know, and you can always *walk away* mentally. Be understanding and tolerant for that's who you are. You are better than a simple-minded judge.

"So what if *he*'s got a nice car? So what if *she* can afford to travel around the world?" There is no point in being jealous because you are as capable as they are, and they define their own success different from the way you define yours. Everyone defines everything in their own way; it's a *perspective* and it's the natural act of judgement. It's when we use it to influence our conscience by stoking its anger and hate is when we begin to misuse it. Learn to immediately spot the signs when you start to roll down the negative side of the hill and stop it *immediately. Snap out of it!* Don't give it a chance to spill everywhere else in your head. It spreads quicker than you think.

The most common mistake we do is to believe that there is not enough success to go around for everybody and that we are all limited to establish a hierarchy. If you took someone to dinner, paid a well spent meal using the money you earned, don't skimp on the feeling of spending it. Sure, it's not pleasing to see your money leave your hands, but if you hang on to that loss of "it was painful to see that cash go," it will ruin the blessing of the entire event, meal and all. I'm not saying to go haphazardly spending copious amounts of cash, I'm saying not to dwell on the insufficiency of it. When life sees that you are mindful of something, it will give you the opportunity of getting more of it. But if your mindfulness is on the discomfort of letting go of that cash, it will give you more of that discomfort. If it sees that you are in no pain in paying the tab and are pleased with the results of your labor instead, it will give you more opportunities to experience similar situations.

Anything you put your mind to,
consciously or subconsciously, will
happen if you continue to believe it.

This is one of the reasons why some of us learn to be greedy. We think there is a limited amount of opportunities (not resources, mind you) to sustain our satisfaction. If you kept replaying *dopamine-inducing* memories in your head frequently of the time you gave to the poor and needy, well guess what? Life will give you *more* opportunities to do so and will supply you with the means provided you willingly give your dedication and trust that you will always be provisioned for, and that life will always find a way. If you enjoyed the memory of embarrassing someone and perversely used it to feel good, well, life will give you more opportunities to repeat it too.

You must trust Life/the Universe/God—*all* is *one*. You are in a relationship with the power that creates worlds. Give that power the honor of believing that it *will* pull through for you in good times and in bad. Just as you trust the best friends you've ever had, so should you trust it even more. That *power* will spoil you, believe it. Its objective is to provide you with continued satisfaction given your commitment, that you know exactly what you want, and that you trust it, *unless* it finds something better for you. If you *flip-flop* with your thoughts and beliefs in it, it won't be successful in *hitting a moving target* to give you what you truly desire. You'd be sending *mixed signals* to your best friend.

I once considered my best friend more than just a typical friend and called him a "body-mover" because he would morbidly joke, "Friends help you move. *Real friends* help you move bodies." That is *exactly* what the Universe is to you—a *body-mover*.

When we talked about believing in an earlier chapter, remember that you can believe positively as much as you can believe negatively. Both types of belief are equally powerful, though it goes without saying that you should choose the former for obvious reasons of benefit. Just as you can achieve insurmountable blessings, you can also achieve insurmountable loss, both of which are led by the same belief system. *I'm telling you*—the universe with its unfathomable wisdom will be your primary sponsor.

Are you familiar with that feeling when you are deeply thanked for something you've given to someone and seeing that person really enjoy and cherish what you've given them? You may have done it when you gave a present for a child's birthday and saw them open it. There it is, that *precious* look on their face, that smile, that laughter and excitement! So genuine and heartfelt. Aren't you compelled to do it again and perhaps even more than before?

Therefore, honor your relationship with the universe through acknowledgement. Just as you would get that *warm fuzzy feeling* when you appreciate receiving a surprise gift from someone, be thankful for the gifts that life gives you—the opportunities, the lessons, the rewards. Say *"thank you"* as often and as profound as you can throughout your day. It doesn't have to be this huge *production* all the time when you say or do it, but you can take my word that it is absolutely appreciated, and I guarantee that like any healthy relationship, the universe will give you more of what you treasure based on how gleefully they are received. In other words, "Be sincere with your thanks."

And here you once thought, "The universe is not a living being. How could it express a reciprocal appreciation?"

Oh, but it *is*! *Life* came from *Life*, remember? Aren't you a product of life? Doesn't life come in many forms, some even beyond our limited scientific deduction? Treat the universe as a being full of life such as yourself. In your lifetime, you will never be considered *alone* no matter how isolated you make yourself to be.

You know what's another form of acknowledgement? *Prayer*.

When you pray, pray with a positive tone. If you are in times of strife and you pray, pray with a trusting tone. The universe knows when you are having a difficult time, and during these times, it hears you even louder. Therefore, present yourself and your intentions to it honorably and maturely. If you cry like a child cries as you make your plea, it won't be able to properly reason with you just like you would find it difficult to reason with an emotionally-compromised child. Even worse—a child with a temper tantrum.

Do you understand the difference between a person begging and a person appealing? Begging means that someone is at the end of their rope, that most, if not all hope is lost. Appealing means that someone is composed and forward-thinking of their request. You typically react different to both, and so does the universe. So be proper. Raise yourself higher. Compose yourself and gather yourself together. One does not wallow in mud and assert pity. Neither does one make an arrogant petition and expect clemency.

Practice being thankful to everything around and in you until it becomes second nature to all that you do. When you wake up, think of something to be thankful for. When you go out and walk, be thankful for at least one thing. "Thank you for *this*. Thank you for *that*." Appreciate, acknowledge, and enjoy what soothes your mind on whatever you are thankful for. Don't be cynical or sarcastic with your *"thank yous."* It shouldn't feel that you're *forced* to say thanks and it should be stated naturally. Not everything is something you *have to* thank for, not especially the things that you don't like (borderline *masochism*). Though sometimes, what you may not like in the beginning, you end up realizing it was something to be thanked for its manifestation. An undesirable event can lead to a desirable one, and a desirable event can lead to more desirable events. Be thankful for the positive outcomes, the opportunities, and whatever lessons you learned from them.

Let's say you took some friends out to dinner and they weren't *exactly* on their best behavior. Maybe they were rude to the wait staff, or were too rowdy at the table, or spilled wine all over your favorite shirt. Wasn't quite the pleasant evening you expected.

Are they still your friends afterwards? Did they offend you personally, or just your personal preferences? Did you at least enjoy the meal? Were they always like this every time you take them out? Look for the opportunity to learn from the situation and adjust accordingly. See things from a different perspective, even from theirs. Always find the good in people. Forgive them but be mindful that they can be a handful to others. Be thankful for the meal and the chance to get together.

You notice a theme?

Everything is connected. I'm not just talking about the relationship between you, the Maker, and all. I'm also talking about how the lessons in each chapter of this book are connected and able to relate to one another. It's a system that's *part of* a bigger system that works *within* an even bigger system. Did a lightbulb just turn on? Let me give you another perspective then:

If you decide to read this book all over again or review some past chapters, you'll notice that the message becomes different than when you read it the previous time. It's like watching a movie once and then watching it again with the *subtitles* on. You somehow know it, parts of it are familiar, but there's an evolved dialogue and message you've never noticed before. Though for the sake of this chapter, let's keep reading.

Make yourself a daily regimen; a recurring recipe for success. For example, as soon as you wake-up in the morning, practice being thankful and appreciative of something, even the smallest things or a memory of something that makes you happy. That's the first thing you think of—not the agenda for the day, not those *things* you have to do later. Just be thankful. Appreciate the fact that you are alive, as basic as that notion may seem. If you can't think of anything else positive, keep lying there until you do. When it comes to wallowing in something positive, you make time for it. When whatever you're appreciative of comes into mind, let it linger a bit, allow that feeling to flow for at least half a minute. Whatever the rest of your agenda is after it will step aside and yield, just let it set the tone for the start of your day, that's *priority one*. If you start your day positive, it will likely end positive. Now that you've set the tone, do what you must do to get ready in the morning. Look forward to the day and what lies ahead. There may be challenges but I guarantee there *will be* opportunities.

It's important to take moments just for yourself. Sometimes, it can become a busy day for you, but there will always be time for even a short pause to be thankful for something. If you are fortunate to have several minutes, find those things you are thankful that happened since the morning and give them a nod of appreciation. Keep your *flag of positivity* waving. Tackle the rest of the day with trust in yourself knowing that no matter what, you'll get through it, the day will end just like any other day, and you will be given another opportunity to make-up for whatever you missed.

Perhaps close to the end of the day or after coming home, practice letting-go of whatever you didn't like that happened the past hours. I'm referring to the ones that really *stood-out* and *stuck* with you, such as the stress you forgot to leave at your workplace or the sting of that individual who *cut you off* in the freeway. If you can or must, take a walk and recite your positive affirmations. Validate to yourself that you are a very capable being and one who can make manifest immeasurable success. You can banish what drags you down and you can replace them with *"memory trophies"* of your great achievements and small wins, or some understanding and forgiveness. Clean the *mental attic* as frequent as you can, keeping it pristine and orderly and bright.

Realize your place in the universe and be grateful that you are part of the most amazing system in the galaxy. Make a peaceful relationship with your subconscious by meditating or just closing your eyes and enjoy a bit of stillness amidst the *ever-moving pace* of the world. Stay still and reflect. Connect with the *bigger picture* or the *larger cause* of your purpose. Don't let the negative things stick to you. Don't let the woes of the day define who you are. Remember the potential of how amazing you can be and what you can do. Let the inner being realize that there is nothing to fear, that it is safe with your stability.

Before going to bed, reflect. Again, be thankful for all the wonderful things in your life, don't skimp on the details. Large or small, they all build you for the better. If you're a person of prayer, pray. Pray as an acknowledgement of your belonging to forces that guide and watch over you and do so sincerely. Not only have you motivated your subconscious all-day, but you have communicated those feelings back to the universe. And as the universe sees it, so shall it respond and give you *more* of the essences of what you are thankful for. It sees that you are sound of mind and that your fortitude is resolute, and it sees you *worthy*.

Whatever has happened in between during the day such as the details of your work, your commute, your tasks for the day, the lessons you learned, the people you've interacted with, and so on, they will all fall under the category of your positive scope and more opportunities will yield to you. You attract more of what you think of, so when you think positively, the opportunities that meet you will likewise be positive. So, line-up with that goodness that flows through you—the force that creates worlds instead of destroying them.

Remember your meditation techniques. Find peace in silence and the order separate from the chaos. Project *more* into the future and dwell *less* on the past. Practice the traits, expectations, and mindset of who you would be like *after* you have attained your goals in life. The universe does not discern whether you have something in your hand already or if you're just imagining it. The universe feeds and responds to your emotions and as I said before, it will spoil you, so give it the proper emotion you project. When you do get to the goals you have set for yourself in life, cherish them and enjoy them. Do *not* be selfish with them or use them to stir jealousy towards others. Be humble with what you have by respecting it, not using it for boisterous expression and waving it all around for all to see. You do not need the affirmative approval from others to be successful and retain it. You need your own self approval and respect, one that reflects itself back to the universe and God.

Never be impatient during your journey because time is irrelevant. Time is not the enemy on how good you can feel about yourself right now. When you are on the path to manifesting whatever your goal is, it's ok to *throttle down*, to slow your pace, there is no requirement to get to the finish line within a finite time because life will always know more than you do and which path you should take along the way. Build your momentum using meditation, mindfulness, and thankfulness. As your momentum becomes stronger, it becomes more difficult to destabilize your trust in the process, and your discipline *will* keep your balance in check.

Impatience is a very engrained process in all of us, especially in this age where most people feel they *have to be* somewhere, want to be somebody, or constantly look for immediate gratification. You know how to deal with your impatience now, however, so we don't need to rehash that lesson. You know how to steer yourself to the positive course when things don't go your way. You also know that if you begin to question yourself, "*Why aren't I there yet,*" it will only re-introduce doubt. Finally, you know that comparing your current state with *your preferred end game* will only cause anxiety. Have fun along the way, openly *rendezvous* with the opportunities, the stages, the experiences, and the *building blocks*.

> It's not just all about the end game;
> much of it is about the journey.

"You are *already* in it." Your positive development is happening as we speak. *The update is in progress.* State your objectives simple and your imagination about the possibilities as wide open as you can spread your wings. When you feel like life is making you wait, remember that it's because it is trying to show you there are potential details you may want to see and a reason for further refinement on your behalf.

When you find doubts in your abilities to complete something, stop and perform a *self-validation*. How would someone who cares about you see you? If you placed yourself in the shoes of a good friend, how would that friend see and appreciate you? Take yourself out of your view, look at yourself from different *angles* using visualization practices. When we become so engrossed with what we do and what we want to accomplish, we tend to get *tunnel vision*. This is also another reason why getting up from your seat at work every now and then is a good thing. From a different scale, it is also good to do something different from your *normal week* when the weekend arrives. Shake it up! If you work hard, play hard.

Years ago, I used to volunteer at the *Monterey Bay Aquarium* in Monterey, California, during the weekends in the *husbandry* department. The Aquarium in Monterey is worth a visit if you get the chance. Although it was an hour-and-a-half commute from where I lived, it never got tiring to enjoy the drive to the coast before the sun rose. I would gleefully get-up at 5:00 in the morning, put on my volunteer uniform, grab my empty 5-gallon water jugs, and head out. The drive was especially soothing because I knew there was adventure ahead, and it made me easily set aside all the hard work I had done that week in the office. By the time I arrived in Monterey, the sun would peek in the distant horizon behind the bay, and it was such a completely different world.

I regarded the Aquarium as my *second home*. Not only was it different from my usual day job behind the desk, but the people who worked there always had a passion for what they did. Even my first weekly task which was to clean the *children's tide pool exhibit* was so far away from the typing and mouse clicking. I would get my hands wet up to my elbows, picking every snail, Decorator Crab, starfish, and seaweed and placing them in a holding bin before draining the water and washing the area. Every now and then, I'd find an unexpected interesting animal such as a stow-away baby octopus making a *run for it* towards the drain or an *Isopod* the size of my thumb, and that was just the beginning. Throughout the day, I'd help with other chores, mop the areas behind the display tanks, and have lunch outside with the seagulls and sparrows. At the end of the day, I would fill my empty tanks with filtered sea water from the bay, so I could take them back home to maintain the water in my small 15-gallon aquarium. The routine never got old.

When I would get back to my office desk on Monday, I always felt I inherited a new experience every Saturday no water cooler talk could top.

"How was your weekend," a colleague would ask. "I saw a movie."

"It was good. I fed a young *Mola Mola* in quarantine," I would happily reply.

The stark perspective was *unfathomable*. No pun intended (and I wish you could've seen their poker faces attempting to decrypt the answer). There it was, however—the self-validation knowing that I made a difference somewhere and something to feel special about, and my mind would easily *teleport* back to Monterey if I needed to remove stress, looking forward to the next time I see my maritime family again.

*Find something you are passionate
about, especially one that benefits others
in the process.*

At least once in your life, make a list of your accomplishments if you haven't done so. It feels reassuring to see your *Curriculum Vitae* of talents and abilities, and it gives you such a unique view on what you are capable of. Think of it as a *trophy cabinet* but for your eyes only, and the reason of why it's good to jot them down is so that when you get stuck with doubt on your abilities in achieving something, you have an *easy-to-read* list that takes you back to your history and shows how much you've progressed. There are hints in there as well from the patterns you observe about your behavior and on your interests that make you learn more about yourself and find direction on what else you may excel in.

We are so full of potential that each soul reading this book has the means to literally change the world for the better, if not conceive the ultimate version of themselves and discover the incredible limitless achievement they can bring forth to the world. It matters little to me what you do with this potential, only that you use it to better yourself and in turn, for the unselfish benefit of those around you. The higher cause I speak of is something we've already covered previously in chapters before. It creates, it builds, it expands, and you are a mechanism of that upward movement. You are an extension of its wings.

Remember to let your *inner being* out every now and then. Let it play and enjoy all that life brings to it. Reprogram yourself to trust, appreciate, and enjoy all the good things, leaving no vacancy for ill will in your heart and in your memory. Say *thank you* often. Mean it and live it! You will be under the guiding power and protection of your friend, the great universe. You will always be connected to it and you will never be alone. There is plenty of room in this life for you and others even if you do not share the same space. The goal is for *everyone* to benefit *everyone*. Fear will make you defensive and reclusive but being wise will help you conquer and gain allies. Everyone has an *inner being* they are trying to protect. See it that way.

Think of your successful future *you*. Visualize it. What would your *future you* tell you? It would probably say this:

"I'm proud of what you can become. Although I am your perceived definition of success right now, I know you can do much better than I did, and I firmly believe that because I am you and I know what you are capable of. I wouldn't trick you or lead you down a misled path because doing so will jeopardize me and we'd only be going in circles. Feel the positivity in you, feel that energy, that potential. Trust that feeling. Don't be afraid to go out and get it! Go after your dreams! I believe you will be great, even *greater* than me, and I would relive my life all over again for you just to see that happen. Keep that up and never let the turbulence along the way buck you from the saddle because your alignment with yourself and with the trust you have towards the universe and the God within you is what *will* get us here and beyond. Remember when there was a time you wanted what you currently have? Well, we made it to *this* amazing level! How about that? Do you hear me? *We made it!*

I'm *always* rooting for you and I love you dearly; to the moon and back a million times forever. Remember me always. I'll be waiting for you here at the finish line and hope to see you go way past it. You are, *and always will be,* part of something much bigger. You and I will always be connected. You will never lose me, I promise. Not to anyone or anything."

Therefore, feel confident everywhere you go. Expect respect as much as you give respect. Expect happiness as much as you give happiness. What you make of your mind is what you make of your home. Where it is, is where your heart is focused on. Find the *real you* and never sell yourself short on any deal.

Learn to fall in love with life all over again. Love is not just a feeling. It is not just the driving force of our positive emotions. Love is what the Universe has been trying to show us from the very beginning. Love is the Universe, Love is God, Love is you. Love is what prompted me to write this book that's dedicated to you: the conduit of Love.

Remember that you do not become stronger nor gain the upper-hand on anyone by withholding love or using it as a bargaining chip. Love is either there or it isn't; its either on or off. Adding a condition to its terms nullifies it. Love is true, limitless, forgiving, and it never fades. True love spans the tests of time and will evolve in levels of appreciation and reciprocation.

It can start with you, dear friend—with you and with others that think similarly. I firmly believe you are as capable as anyone else to redefine a new way of thinking, of reasoning, reacting, and live in a level far above the person you see yourself today. Always remember that you are a co-creator of your goals and anything you want to make manifest; you are not just a requester. You create an image of what you want, and trust that the universe will try to fulfill that image, if not find something better. Be thankful, learn to forgive more, exercise patience, appreciation, differences in perspective, and most especially, *believe*. Let go of who you've defined yourself and how others have defined you in the past. Become the best version of yourself knowing fully that you are limitless and internally divine. Surrender to accept what the universe wants to give you and realize that your potential is supported by overwhelming positive abundance. Be kind, stay kind, do kind. Be brave and never fear to discover what is beyond and where life beckons you because there is no other way from here but up.

Have an amazing odyssey; the journey of a lifetime. Life will no longer be the same for you and you can certainly make things better.

Now go—*spread your wings and fly*!

Peace be with you always!

Dedicated to our angels in heaven, the ones who live among us, and the ones we keep in our hearts.

Angels do watch over you.